Mosaic Made Easy

Mosaic Made Easy

Alice Vinten

NEW HOLLAND

This edition published in 2015 by New Holland Publishers Pty Ltd
London • Sydney • Auckland

Unit 009, The Chandlery 50 Westminster Bridge Road London SE1 7QY UK
1/66 Gibbes Street Chatswood NSW 2067 Australia
218 Lake Road Northcote Auckland New Zealand

www.newhollandpublishers.com

A record of this book is held at the British Library and the National Library of Australia.

ISBN 9781742576138

Managing Director: Fiona Schultz
Publisher: Diane Ward
Editor: Simona Hill
Typesetter: Peter Guo
Production Director: Olga Dementiev
Printer: Toppan Leefung Printing Ltd

10 9 8 7 6 5 4 3 2 1

Keep up with New Holland Publishers on Facebook
www.facebook.com/NewHollandPublishers

Contents

Introduction: Mosaic and Me   7

Mosaic Techniques   10

The Projects   27

Simple Striped Coaster   29

Vintage Refrigerator Magnet   33

Garden Apples   36

Honey Bee Coaster   40

Rainbow Butterflies   44

China Heart   49

Bunting   55

Tea-Light Holder   61

Garden Pot   65

Sun Circle House Number   68

Bird-Shaped Jewel Box   75

Circular Jewel Box   80

Christmas Bauble   86

Christmas Tree   92

Owl Lantern   99

Floral Tray   107

3D Heart   112

Meadow in a Bowl   118

Peacock Vase   124

Gaudi-Inspired Clock   132

Suppliers   138

Templates   142

About the Author   144

Introduction

Mosaic and Me

My passion for mosaic started more than ten years ago, when I visited Park Güell, Barcelona, in Spain. Park Güell was designed by Gaudi and is considered to be one of his major works. As I gazed in awe at the sparkling beauty of that artist's mosaic artistry, I thought 'I need to try this'. Back at home, I promptly ordered some medium density fibreboard (MDF), mosaic tiles, a tile cutter and some glue. And I was off. My first mirror was a little wonky, but I loved it (and I sold it at my first craft fair!). As the years have gone by my technique has become honed and my style more detailed.

Mosaic is a beautiful medium to work with. It is both strong and infinitely delicate all at once. What is more, it has the potential to last a lifetime. I have been creating mosaic art for more than 10 years and have sold large commissioned mirrors around the world. I have sold my work at craft fairs and online. My mosaics have been displayed in art galleries, my signature 3D hearts have received praise from delighted customers, and my work has won prizes.

All the designs in this book can be tweaked to your own tastes and to suit your own décor. You can choose the colour and materials for your mosaics, or you can follow my suggestions. It's totally up to you. I will provide you with templates and detailed guides, but if you want to get creative and add your own personality to the designs, then nothing would please me more. I have taken my personal experiences of working with mosaic design, the techniques

I have learnt and all the tips that I have developed along the way, and poured them into this book. From the first make to the last, each design will develop your skills.

The projects that feature here have been designed with beginners in mind, but they are detailed enough to keep those of you who have tried mosaic before happy too. A complete novice can pick up this book, start at the beginning and work their way through to the end, becoming a competent mosaic craftsperson along the way. The designs range from the more simple projects at the beginning, to decidedly intricate and challenging projects toward the end. However, if you're just desperate to start in the middle, or even jump in with both feet at the Gaudi-Inspired Clock, I'm not going to stop you. I'll just be delighted that you're enjoying it.

As you progress through this book you will become more confident at cutting and placing your tiles. There is nothing more satisfying than cleaning away the grout to reveal a stunning piece of artwork. And that is exactly what each piece will be: Art. Whether you are making a plant pot or a tea-light holder, a wall clock or a hanging heart, each piece will be a part of you. Your time, your care, your patience and your skill. What better way to decorate a home than to fill it with gorgeous items you have created yourself. And what nicer gift to give than something lovingly made with your own hands?

Please read through the next chapter, Mosaic Techniques, before you begin to work your way through the projects. This will give you all the information you need about cutting tiles, gluing them into place and grouting. It also details some important safety aspects. Mosaic is a wonderful medium, but it does need to be treated with respect.

Mosaic Techniques

SAFETY FIRST

You will be working with many different types of glass, tile and pottery throughout this book. Each medium 'cuts' in a certain way, each one splinters differently, and even the most experienced mosaic artist has cut a finger at some point. Mostly these small injuries are no worse than paper cuts, but please take care that you always clear down your work station after a cutting session. This is especially important if you will be working somewhere where small children will be playing. I have a nifty little hand-held vacuum that I keep next to my cutting bench, which is great for sucking up all the small glass particles after I've finished working.

There is a small risk of flying glass when you cut your tiles. I would like to get you through this book with both eyeballs intact. That brings me to my first piece of equipment:

EQUIPMENT

Safety Goggles

I know from experience that goggles are not necessarily the most popular crafting accessory. Nobody wants to wear them. Let's face it, you're not going to look sexy while sporting large plastic goggles, an apron (probably smeared in grout), with tile glue stuck under your finger nails and a feverish look of creative mania in your eyes.

Apron

You'll also need an apron. When we work on glass you will be using strong glue and I know, from bitter experience, that it doesn't come off brand new jeans that you couldn't be bothered to change out of because you were so overcome with artistic inspiration that you just started wildly cutting and sticking… ahem. An apron is important to protect you and your clothing from tiny glass particles. The particles aren't dangerous, but they do tend to irritate sensitive skin, so it's always best to rinse your hands after cutting your tiles.

Tile Nippers

Arguably, the most important tool for a mosaic artist is a pair of tile cutters. I have always used wheeled tile nippers and have found them both reliable and suitable for all the pieces I have made. They vary in price and quality, but you can certainly get a very decent pair at an affordable price.

Additionally grout sponges and a lint-free cloth for polishing (I use a cut-up car leather/shammy) and a flexible plastic

I have always used Leponitt wheeled nippers and have found them to be solid and reliable. It is worth investing in a quality pair of nippers if you are serious about mosaic.

spatula are essential. Non-scratch nylon scouring pads are also quite useful for cleaning off grout.

MATERIALS

There are many different types of mosaic tiles to choose from, which is great if you love designs that are rich in colour and texture. In the next section I will describe each type in more depth.

Small triangles of mirror and pink glitter tile, with larger triangles of iridescent tile, in a range of purple hues.

Originally a china plate, these tiles were made by first smashing the plate with a hammer, then cutting the pieces into small, roughly triangular, shapes with my nippers.

Mosaic Tiles

In this book we will be using four main types of tiles, as well as jewellery, broken china and glass pebbles. The tiles we use are iridescent tiles, glitter tiles, opaque glass tiles and transparent tiles. Each has completely different qualities that add immeasurably to mosaic designs. I'll start by telling you a bit about my favourites; the iridescent tiles.

Iridescent tiles have a shimmering quality. They change colour in every light and often have a 'petrol-like' sheen across the top layer. They are usually made in small squares of 1.5 cm ($^5/_8$ in) and are easy to cut. They seldom splinter, and are perfect for cutting into small triangles and little details. I usually find myself adding at least some iridescent tiles to every piece I make: I just can't resist them.

Another type of tile I use frequently is the glitter tile. The name says it all. Sparkly, bright and funky, these tiles really do jazz up a project. They are widely available and growing in popularity. They are usually made in squares of 2 cm (¾ in), and are clear glass with a glitter film on the back. Again, they are relatively easy to cut, although they are ever so slightly thicker than the iridescent tiles, and therefore need a bit more pressure applied when cutting them. A small amount of glitter tiles go a long way, and although I use them often, I am careful not to use too many in any one design for fear of making it gaudy.

Transparent tiles also feature in a number of projects in this book. They are excellent for any designs where you would like the light to diffuse through a glass base. Similar to the glitter tiles, they are also usually 2 cm (¾ in) square, and often have ridged lines across the back to aid with grip. Transparent tiles are more delicate than the glitter and iridescent tiles, and are therefore more prone to splintering. They cut very easily, but you have to be extra careful when positioning your tile nippers. It's so easy to create a 'wonky' cut with these tiles. I would always advise you to cut *across* the

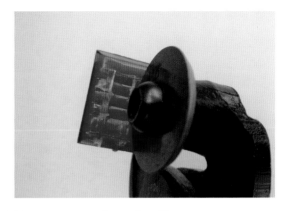

Red opaque glass tile. Always cut across the lines where possible.

lines on the back where possible; they seem to cut better this way.

The staple of all mosaic work is the opaque glass tile. These come in a wide range of shades, shapes and sizes. They are robust and easy to cut, slightly more prone to splintering than the other tiles, but with practice at cutting this won't be a problem.

Cutting Mosaic Tiles

Nippers are simple to use. You take the tile you wish to cut, and place it between the wheels at the point where you wish to cut it. Now squeeze the handles together

Halves.

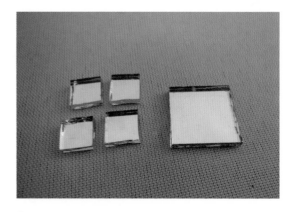

Square quarters.

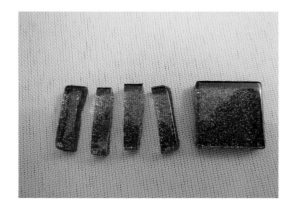

Long quarters.

8ths.

until they grip the tile, then continue to add pressure smoothly and firmly until the tile snaps. I often use one hand to squeeze the handles, and one to cup around the nippers to catch the tile. If you don't do this the tile pieces can end up flying off in any direction! Before you start making your projects you may want to practise a few simple cuts, to get you started.

Throughout the book I will be describing to you the shapes or fractions you will need to cut your tiles into. The main cuts you

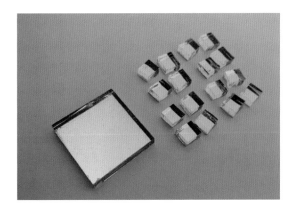

16ths.

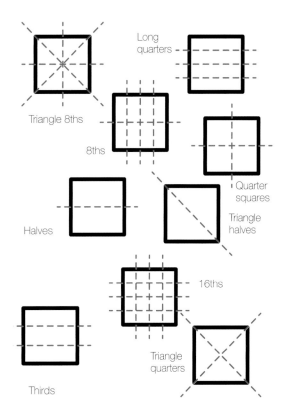

Diagram showing various cuts that can be made into square tiles. Cuts shown in dashed lines.

will need to make to create the items in this book are listed here, with a description of how to cut them:

Long Quarters: Take a square tile and cut it in half. Then cut each half in half again lengthways = 4 long lengths.

Quarters: Take a square tile and cut it in half. Cut each half in half: 4 small squares.

8hs: Take a square tile and cut it in half. Cut again into quarters. Now cut each quarter in half: 8 small rectangles.

16ths: Create 8ths as above. Cut each in half: 16 smaller squares.

You will also need to make diagonal cuts for many of the projects. This is essentially the same as cutting a straight line, except that you have to place the tile between the nipper wheels at the desired angle. Diagonal

Position of tile in cutters to achieve a diagonal cut.

Cutting square quarters into diagonal halves, to achieve triangular 8ths.

cuts are more likely to 'go wonky' so you will need a little practice with this.

For every project, I have allowed a few extra tiles to compensate for mistakes. Always have a little tub or box with you to put any small 'off-cuts' into when you have finished. Never waste unused tiles. You can sort them into colours later on, or, when the box is full, you can enjoy making a colourful project with all the extra pieces! I put my 'off-cuts' into jars. Not only does it make for a very colourful craft shelf, I often find myself rummaging through them for that perfect piece.

Smashing China

From teapots, cups, saucers and plates, if it's old, unloved but looks pretty, then grab it, smash it and use it! I am constantly on the look out for pretty vintage china. I can't pass a charity shop without going in.

When you smash pottery you must wear safety goggles. Place your chosen pot, plate or whatever it is, into a plastic bag (double this up so you actually have two bags, as sharp edges create holes!) and loosely gather the ends together, so that nothing can fly out. Now get a big hammer and break up the pottery. Try not

Once you have smashed your china into manageable pieces, use your nipper to cut the shape and size that you need.

to worry about enjoying this part so much, it's normal.

Once you have broken your pottery into several pieces, use tile nippers to cut them up until you have the sizes you need. Before you start to clip away, however, take a moment to look for any particularly attractive details that you may want to single out for use in a design. You can cut around these (birds, flowers, brightly coloured details, etc) and save them to use as the centre of your creations (maybe for the Vintage Refrigerator Magnets, or China Hearts).

Using broken pottery in mosaics has been around for years and is now so popular, that you can actually buy pottery tiles ready cut online.

Glue

In this book we will be using two types of glue. The first is a standard adhesive, available in every DIY store, that will instantly grab your tiles and hold them in place, while still allowing you to adjust them if you need to before it fully dries. Any multi-purpose adhesive, tile glue, or any non-solvent based strong adhesive that is adjustable as it dries is suitable. It is usually white or beige and can be sanded down once it has dried. It dries very hard and is ideal for keeping tiles in place during grouting. It is generally cheaper than tile glue, but if you prefer to use tile glue then this is also suitable. I use this glue for all of my projects, except for those where I am working directly onto glass.

As this glue dries so hard, it is important to remember to wipe away any excess after each stage. I will remind you to do this throughout the book. It is such an important point to remember in order to avoid positioning problems later on in your projects. I usually use a small grout scraper, or anything long and pointy (small plastic spatula, end of a pencil, fingernail) to remove excess glue as I work.

The other type of glue I use is a multi-purpose contact adhesive, suitable for use on glass. There are a few things to remember when using this type of glue. Firstly, it's very sticky (sounds obvious, I know) and can be hard to remove from the surface of the tiles since it dries like rubber. Therefore, if you end up with glue on your fingers, take the time to wash them before going any further. This will prevent sticky fingerprints on your finished piece. If soap doesn't work, try white spirit.

Secondly, this glue is hazardous. If you are using a large amount of it over a long period, then make sure you work in a well ventilated area. It is thick and gloopy,

Different grout colours will affect the way your final piece looks, I often use black grout, but it is simply a matter of personal preference.

and usually colourless and transparent. Once you are ready to start sticking, apply the glue quite thickly, as it will need to get a good grip on the tiles. Work in small sections, i.e., one line of tiles at a time. It will dry quickly, but will give you time to adjust tile position if you need to. When working on glass, there is always opportunity for tiles to slip. This is especially the case when working on a vertical glass surface, so always take time to look back over your most recent steps to readjust, if necessary.

Grout

White and black grout are used in the projects I have designed for this book. The colour you choose can have a huge impact on the final appearance of a mosaic piece. In some of the projects, I have provided you with a photo of the finished piece in both colour grouts, so that you can choose

I often use small pieces of cardboard boxes for intricate grouting. Always push the grout into and around every detail.

which you prefer. In others I have simply suggested one colour grout. This is because I think that the design would not suit the other grout. However, as always, feel free to use whatever grout you prefer.

Standard grout in tubs, which is available at all DIY shops, is fine for most mosaics. If you will only be grouting here and there, with large gaps of time in-between, then it is best to buy grout in powder form, and mix up the desired amount as you need it, following the packet instructions. If you buy ready-made grout in a tub it will start to dry out as soon as it's opened.

There are many tools to apply grout. Most large DIY stores have a selection at inexpensive prices. You can use grout spatulas, kitchen spatulas, trowels, basically anything that is flexible enough to spread the grout evenly. I often find myself using torn up bits of firm cardboard (card stock), as I can cut it to the size I require; it's flexible, and I am always surrounded by cardboard boxes for some reason.

Grouting is an essential part of any mosaic project. It doesn't matter how beautiful your design is, if you get the grouting wrong the whole piece could be ruined. Luckily, it's a technique easily mastered and with my practical advice, you'll be happily grouting away in no time.

Push your grout in every direction when applying it. If you only smooth over the grout from left to right you will end up with holes once it is dry. Try and visualise that you are filling all the little cracks in your project with your grout. Push it up, down, left and right and back again. You want it to be smooth and even when it is finished. Push the grout into all the nooks and crannies. Don't worry about the excess, this can be wiped away when you've finished. *Always* put a lot of newspaper down when you grout. Especially if you favour black grout, as I do. It gets everywhere.

It can be tricky to grout the edges of some projects, for example, the rim of your tea-lights and vase. I have found that grouting from both directions helps to ensure even coverage. So you can push the grout up from *under* the edge, as well as down *over* the edge. I often gently wipe around my edges with my fingers, to smooth out any gaps or bulges. If the glass is particularly sharp on an edge, then it is often best to give it a rub with some fine grade sandpaper (glasspaper) before grouting.

When using broken china in projects, you will often find that you have depth differences between your tiles and your china. If this is the case, continue grouting as normal, remembering to push your grout into the design firmly and in all directions. I then use my finger to gently wipe away the grout that has gathered between the china and the tiles. This means there will be less grout to clean off later, when your grout is dry. If you don't feel comfortable using your bare finger, you could stretch a very slightly damp piece of shammy leather across your fingertip, or use a traditional grouting sponge. Always remember to wipe away your excess grout, while it is still wet.

In this book we will start with mostly flat projects, made using even tiles. Grouting these projects is relatively simple. However, when you come to the 3D makes nearer the end of the book, the grouting becomes a little more tricky. The primary thing to remember is to push your grout in everywhere. With the vase and bowl projects you will be grouting curved surfaces and will need to make sure to spread grout evenly around the curves, in all directions, to ensure every gap is filled.

TROUBLE SHOOTING AND TIPS

• Always check over your piece and adjust any tiles that may have been knocked or look slightly wonky. The glue should give you bit of time to play with before it sets hard.

• If you find that a tile has dried wonky, use a flat-head screwdriver to prise it off. Do this as gently as possible, so as not to crack the tile. Scrape off the glue underneath and re-apply.

• If you find that a tile dislodges as you are grouting (this does happen occasionally) then just squash it into the grout and smooth over it well. It should be absolutely fine once the grout has set.

• If your tiles have lines across the back, always make your first cut *across* the lines. Your tiles will cut better this way, I promise.

• Scrape away excess glue before progressing to the next stage. This is especially important if you are planning on leaving your project for a while and coming back to it later.

• Keep a box with you while working, for 'off-cuts' and spare tiles.

• Work in a well ventilated area when using glue on glass.

• Push grout in all directions so that every crack is filled.

• Remember to take a break! It is easy to get caught up in a project and unconsciously hunch over it, moving your face closer and closer, until you are curled over into a very unnatural position. This does nothing for your shoulders and neck, let alone your posture! Take regular breaks during your projects. Get up and move about. If you find that your neck and shoulders feel tense, try a few shoulder rolls, backwards and forwards, to loosen them up.

UP-CYCLING, RE-PURPOSING AND SOURCING INEXPENSIVE MATERIALS

I was recently asked to define up-cycling. After a short ponder, I explained that up-cycling was a bit like re-cycling, but with a fundamental difference. Recycling is taking something used and unwanted, cleaning it, blasting it, squishing it, pulping it, and then making something new out of the pulp. Up-cycling is about taking something used and unwanted, cleaning it, fixing it, embellishing it and giving it a bit of love, so that you end up with something new and usable once more.

You would be forgiven for thinking that making mosaics would be a pricey hobby. One look at those glittering tiles and you can already feel your purse strings tightening. However, there are many ways that you can save money.

I love to use broken or unwanted china in my designs. It gives me such a sense of pleasure to take something beautiful, that has become old and unwanted, and give it a new lease of life by transforming it. There is, of course, the added bonus of the cost! You can pick up plates and cups, vases and saucers in a variety of colours and designs for very small amounts of money in most local charity shops. If you speak to the staff, they may well save the chipped or broken ones for you! The only thing to remember is to check the thickness of the china before you buy. Mosaic tiles are 4 mm ($^3/_{16}$ in) in depth, so you'll want to try and find pottery of a similar depth. You can use china that is slightly thicker than your tiles, this often gives a nice texture to your work. Too thick, however, and the final mosaic can end up looking bulky.

Regularly pop into your local vintage shops, junk stores and house clearance shops. If you get to know the people who work there then you are more likely to get a good deal. These places are often filled to the brim with little gems that you can pick up for pennies (or cents). Plus, these places often suffer breakages, and they'd prefer to sell them to you for a fraction of the price than lose out altogether. Specifically keeping mosaics in mind, look for small tables with pretty legs, animal sculptures, photo frames, glasses and bowls. All of these items lend themselves very well to being covered in tiles.

Remember to bargain. I used to avoid asking for discounts simply because I couldn't bear the thought of being embarrassed if the answer was no. Thankfully, over the years I have become braver and now I'll *always* try to knock something off the marked price. Honestly, shop workers expect this, rarely batting an eyelid when I ask. Simply asking, 'Is there anything you can do about the price?' will often garner some sort of discount. If you're feeling bolder, why not try starting at a price of your choosing? Always start lower than your maximum budget, so that you can move upwards. The exception to

the rule of 'always barter' is surely charity shops where it's probably best avoided.

One area where you really can't cut the cost of mosaic is the tiles. This must be true, right? Not necessarily. Rather than going directly to a large craft shop, shopping online for tiles will drastically cut your cost. Websites often have great deals on tiles. Another great way of saving money on tiles is to pop into your local tiling or bathroom/kitchen shops. You will find that they have large amounts of stock 'out the back', which has either not sold or been taken off the shop floor for some reason. There is no harm in asking if they will sell you these tiles at a discounted rate. I was once given 10 whole sheets of mosaic tiles (that's 250 tiles per sheet) for just £1 a sheet. The man couldn't sell them as they had gone out of fashion in bathrooms, but, luckily for me, were perfect for mosaics! It's experiences like this that teach you to always ask for a deal. The worst thing they can say is no!

Not only can you source cheap tiles and china, but also jewellery. Charity shops often have strings of beads, necklaces and pretty bracelets available for really low amounts. The jewellery itself may not be to your taste, but if the beads are colourful, brightly patterned or have any redeeming features at all, then they can be used in a mosaic design. The act of adding jewellery to a mosaic instantly turns it into a more tactile object. Beads add sparkle, glamour and depth to a finished design.

Now that we have discussed the equipment you will need, the techniques that you will learn and sourcing your materials for less, we can move on to the exiting part. The making.

Many items found at charity shops are ideal for up-cycling using mosaic. These include vases, picture frames, coasters and small animal ornaments. Jam jars and wooden off-cuts are also great.

The Projects

Simple Striped Coaster

This simple striped design is a perfect starter project for anyone new to mosaics. You can buy blank wooden coasters from craft suppliers, or recycle a charity shop find, using an existing coaster as the base for your mosaic design. This design is covered in brightly coloured iridescent, glitter and mirrored tiles, using mosaic tiles cut into long and square quarters. Learning to cut tiles is an essential skill for making mosaics. The smaller you can cut the tiles, the more detailed and intricate your designs will become.

You will need

Wooden or plain coaster base (10.5 cm/4¼ in square)

20 green iridescent tiles

4 mirror tiles

2 purple glitter tiles

2 green transparent tiles

2 purple opaque tiles

1 lilac opaque tile

1)   Cut the 20 green iridescent tiles in half. Apply a line of glue along one edge and corner of the coaster. Place two tiles at right angles to each other on one corner of the coaster. Set them together so that they form a square edge. Continue placing border tiles until one side is complete.

2)   Continue around the border. End each row with a complete tile, so that the design looks neat. If you need to fill a gap with a smaller tile, add this smaller tile to the middle of the row as it will blend in better. Scrape away any excess glue before continuing – use a thin plastic tool or your fingernail.

3)   To fill in the body of the coaster, first cut the four mirror tiles into quarters. Set four pieces aside. Apply a line of glue and place the remaining quarters on two opposite sides, just inside the border tiles.

Trim a quarter square, if necessary, to help the tiles fit.

4)   Cut the two purple glitter tiles into long quarters. Apply a line of glue on the coaster inside the mirror tiles. Place the tiles on the inside edge of the mirror tiles.

5)   Cut the two green transparent tiles into long quarters and place them inside the purple tiles. Add another row of green iridescent half tiles. Work from each end of the line into the centre. Trim the centre tile to fit. Cut the two purple opaque tiles into long quarters. Apply a line of these next.

6)   Take the four mirror quarters set aside earlier and cut each in half. Place these along the middle of the coaster.

7)   Complete the rest of the coaster reversing the pattern already set out. Leave to set for at least 12 hours.

8) I used white grout to fill the gaps between the mosaic tiles. Refer to the Techniques chapter for grouting instructions. Roughly clean away the excess grout. Set the coaster aside for at least 12 hours before cleaning it.

9) Give the coaster a thorough clean and polish.

Tip: *When applying border tiles, always place the rounded edge of the tile on the edge of the coaster. This will ensure that there are no sharp edges on your finished piece.*

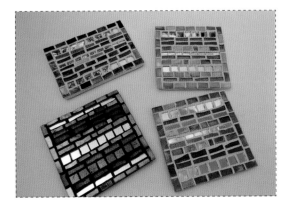

Here you can see the difference between the white and black grout on these finished coasters. Choose whichever you prefer.

Vintage Refrigerator Magnet

These vintage-style refrigerator magnets add a design accent to a kitchen and a stylish means of holding important papers together. You could adapt this design to wear as a scarf pin, or attach it to a long necklace thong and wear it as a vintage pendant, if you like. Pendant fixings and brooch backs can be purchased online.

I have chosen some beautiful old china that I found in a local junk shop for my design. It features pretty birds, lots of colour and a busy pattern.

You will need

5 cm (2 in) diameter wooden circles

Magnets

Broken china with a pretty vintage pattern

3 iridescent tiles in complementary shades

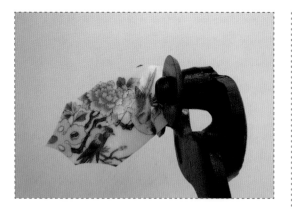

1)   Break the china into pieces (see the cutting information in the Techniques section). Choose a pretty detail for the centre of the mosaic. It can be any shape. Trim it to less than 2 x 2 cm (¾ x ¾ in).

2)   Place the china motif next to the wood circle to check that it will fit. If it is too large keep nipping away at the edge with tile cutters until it is small enough. It should have at least 1 cm (³⁄₈ in) empty space all around the edge for the border. Put a thick blob of glue in the centre of the wood circle and press the tile onto it.

3)   For the border, cut the iridescent tiles into quarters, then cut each quarter in half. Place a thin line of glue all around the edge of the central motif. Add a border tile ensuring its edge is in line with the edge of the wood circle. Keep adding tiles until the border is complete.

4)   Now fill in the rest of the shape. Cut the china pieces into small random

shapes and then places as many as you can into the circle. Set the magnet aside to dry for at least 12 hours.

5) Since this shape is very small it won't need much grout to fill the gaps. I often use a torn piece of sturdy cardboard to grout small projects. Using the cardboard or small grout spatula, press the grout into the design, taking care to grout inward across all the edges. Wipe the excess grout away with your fingers or a slightly damp shammy leather. Leave to dry completely before polishing.

6) Using strong glue, stick the magnet to the back of the wooden circle. If you would like a really professional finish, use paint to coat the edges and back surface of the magnet.

Tip: *Borders create a professional look and give your magnets a clean finish.*

Garden Apples

Everyone can have an apple tree in their garden with these fabulous hanging apples. These would also look great strung together across a fence. Alternatively, they make great hanging decorations for the kitchen.

Using a mixture of new red tiles and broken china, these apples are quaint and striking all at once. The red glitter tiles add plenty of sparkle. This project will help develop mosaic skills: instead of cutting tiles into strict fractions, here they're cut randomly to achieve a 'crazy paving' effect.

You will need

Wooden apple shape with leaf detail and stem with hole for hanging
   (9 x 9 cm or 3½ x 3½ in)

Broken china or pottery (preferably with a green or red pattern)

4 red opaque tiles

4 red glitter tiles

4 red transparent tiles

1 iridescent green tile

1)   Cut the tiles and broken china to roughly the same size and into random shapes. Apply a line of glue all the way around the edge of the wooden apple.

2)   Choose the edge tiles first. They will determine the finished shape of the apple, so make sure you choose carefully. If you can, place any rounded edges of the tiles on the edge of the wooden shape. (You can always use fine grade sandpaper (glasspaper) once the design is complete to file any sharp sides. Position the tiles around the edge of the apple. Mix up the hues and tiles.

3)   Once you have placed the border tiles, fill in the rest. Place the rest of your tiles on the wood, spacing the colours and tile types so that you have a good mix across the design. Cut the tiles to fit into the spaces as you work in toward the centre. You may end up with a few small gaps after placing all your tiles. Cut some pieces into small triangles to fill these.

4) To shape the leaf, use clippers to nibble away small pieces of tile until you have a rough leaf shape. Keep referring to your wooden apple shape to judge the required size, or if you prefer, draw the leaf shape on a mosaic tile and draw around it using a marker pen. Clip the shape to the drawn line until you are happy with the shape. Stick it in place and leave to dry overnight.

5) Grout the mosaic following the instructions in the Technique chapter. White grout will set off the red colour perfectly and keep the design light and fresh. Remember to push the grout into the edges of the apple, as well as into the top. To grout around the leaf detail, simply take some grout on your finger and push it all around the edges of the leaf shape, until it is smooth. Wipe off all excess grout then set aside to dry completely.

6) Use a slightly damp grout sponge to scrub off the excess. Polish the apples and then paint around the edges, if you like.

Honey Bee Coaster

In this small scale project, you'll learn to create motifs, in this case bees, by cutting tiles to precise shapes. This project also requires you to follow a pattern. These coasters will look great anywhere in the house, from a sunny kitchen to a colourful dining room. Four of them tied with a ribbon would be a great gift for a friend.

You will need:

Square coaster or blank coaster base (10.5 cm or 4¼ in square)

14 iridescent green tiles

1 yellow opaque tile

1 gold glitter tile

1 orange opaque tile

1 silver or mirror tile

2 black opaque tiles

25 blue transparent tiles

1)   Start by creating the border. Cut the iridescent green tiles in half. Begin by forming a right angle with the first two tiles, at the corner of the coaster, positioning the rounded edge of the tiles so that they are on the edge.

2)   Continue to place your tiles around the border. Wipe any excess glue as you go.

3)   To create the honey bees, take the black, orange, yellow and glitter gold tiles and cut them into long quarters. Arrange five tile quarters, alternating the stripes, so that the body has three coloured tiles interspaced by two black tiles.

4)   To create the oval body shape, trim the end tiles so that they reduce in length from the middle of the bee. Cut approximately 2–3 mm (1/8 in) from the end of each black tile. Cut the end tiles in half lengthways. Make three bees.

5)   Position the bees on the coaster, placing them a few millimetres away from the border. Each bee will have wings so

allow space for those too. Apply glue in a rough bee shape and place the tiles.

6) Choose a tile for the wings. I chose silver. Cut the tile diagonally into quarters to yield four triangles. Now cut each triangle in half to create small triangles. Don't worry if they are not perfectly even, it's this variety that makes the designs so special.

7) Place the wings on the coaster, leaving space around them for some blue tiles.

8) Fill in the remaining space with blue tiles. Cut the tiles randomly. Once you have a pile of them, start placing them around the bees. Take some pointy triangles and fill in around the wings first in a 'crazy' paving pattern.

9) Once you have filled around the wings, start to line up tiles around the border. Line the straight edges along the border so that your design looks neat. Fill in the rest of the coaster and leave it overnight to dry.

10) Grout the tile following the instructions in the Technique chapter. Scrape the grout along the sides of the coaster to create a smooth edge. Wipe off the excess grout with a sponge or your fingers.

11) Polish the Honey Bee Coaster. For a really smart look, paint around the edges in a complementary colour.

Tip: *Don't worry if your coaster base is slightly rounded at the corners, you can still create a square corner with your tiles. The grout will support the corners.*

Rainbow Butterflies

I love rainbows. I love butterflies. So I decided to indulge my passion and create something awesome. These butterflies would look great strung in a row across a child's bedroom, dotted around the garden or simply hung inside as a decoration. They are simple to make, with all the tiles being cut the same way. The colours are bright and fun, with a few glitter tiles added for good measure.

You will need

Wooden craft butterfly shapes, with holes for hanging (roughly 8 cm/3 in) across)

2 red opaque tiles

2 yellow opaque tiles

2 pink glitter tiles

2 iridescent green tiles

1 orange opaque tile

2 purple opaque tiles

2 blue opaque tiles

1) Cut all the tiles into eight pieces. You can either cut them all up before you start, or cut them as you work. Put a line of glue along the top of the wings on the base. Place red tiles on the glue line, ensuring that they are straight and evenly spaced.

2) Put a blob of glue in the centre of the butterfly's body and place a yellow tile on it. Then apply a line of glue underneath the red tiles on each side. Apply the yellow tiles.

3) The blue tiles are applied next, and to the bottom of the shape, so that we don't leave too much space between tiles at the top, causing us to run out of room at the base. Place a line of glue running down from the centre of the body out to the bottom of the wings. Place your blue tiles.

4) Apply a line of glue underneath the yellow tiles. Position the pink glitter tiles. If you find yourself with a gap of more than 3–4 mm ($1/8$ in), cut a tile to fit.

5) Fill in the top wing with green tiles. Fill the area with glue and arrange the tiles to fit. Place two orange tiles underneath the green section for a bright divide between the top and bottom wings.

6) Cover the remaining wood with glue. Fill any gaps with purple tiles. Leave to dry overnight.

7) Grout the butterflies, holding them by their antennae while you work, to prevent the small wooden details from being plugged with grout. Wipe off the excess grout before setting them aside to dry.

8) Give the butterflies a scrub and polish. String them with pretty ribbon or bright embroidery thread and hang them up. Paint around the edges in a bright coloured paint, if you like.

China Heart

These hearts are so pretty and, as they're small, they're quick and easy to make. The current trend for hanging hearts all over the home, from windows to door handles and anything that stays still long enough, shows no sign of slowing.

For an added decorative bonus, I decided to découpage the rear of my heart before I added the tiles. It adds a nice touch to the finished item. Alternatively, painting the rear is also really easy and looks just as nice.

You will need

Wood 'primitive heart with hole' (10 cm/4 in) long)

1 blue glass pebble

1 mirror tile

4 iridescent blue tiles

Broken china

Ribbon, for hanging

1)   Place the blue pebble in the centre of the wooden heart, about 3 mm ($^1/_8$ in) below the hole. Use an ample blob of glue to hold it in place, you can always wipe away the excess later, or leave it where it is and use it for the next step.

2)   Cut the mirror tile into 16ths. Place these tiny squares around the pebble in a circle. Start at the top, in the centre, and work your way around.

3)   To make the border, cut the blue iridescent tiles into 8ths. Apply a thin line of glue to the base of the heart. Place the first tile at the tip and so that the rounded corner of the tile is facing out.

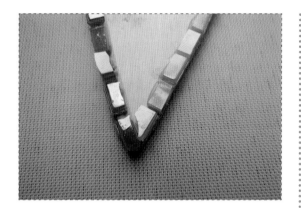

4) Continue to add the border tiles, making sure they are placed in line with the edge of the heart and evenly spaced. When you get to the last tile, you will need to make a slanted cut to finish the point of the heart. Simply hold the tile between two fingers and place it, at the desired angle, into the clippers. Close the clippers gently to hold the tile in place, then cup your hand around them and snap the tile. Place the final tile so that it meets the first.

5) Now fill in the remaining space with broken china, trimming each piece so that you have random shaped, small pieces. Choose a pointed piece to place at the bottom tip of the heart, and then place the larger pieces around the edges, or wherever you can fit them. Once you have placed five or six larger pieces in the heart, you will need to start cutting the china to fill in the gaps. Once your heart is complete, set it aside to dry overnight.

6) Start grouting the shape in the centre, pushing your grout in around the stone so that the mirror tiles are covered. Don't worry about covering the hole at the top as we will re-open it later. Scrape around the stone in both directions to ensure that every space is filled. Immediately wipe off any excess grout from the mirror tiles, then continue to grout the rest of the heart. Once the face of the heart is grouted, turn the heart on its side and go around the edges, pushing in and down as you go. Wipe off the excess grout and set aside to dry.

7) Once the mosaic is dry, scrub off the remaining grout. Take a small 'cross-head' screwdriver and screw down into the grout on top of the hole. Using gentle pressure punch through the hole. Thread through a ribbon for hanging the heart.

Bunting

Bunting is an ever popular decoration for the home and garden and I absolutely love it. I have stepped away from the more traditional fabric and paper bunting with this idea. I wanted to create a stunning design that will last for summer after summer, and party after party. The combination of neutral tones, pottery, mirror tiles and a dash of glitter make these a winner. All you need to string them together is some pretty ribbon.

You will need

Wooden triangle, 12 x 15 cm (4¾ x 6 in) long, with two holes at the top

10 iridescent beige tiles

4 mirror tiles

3 pink glitter tiles

5 iridescent pink tiles

China, cut into small rough triangles

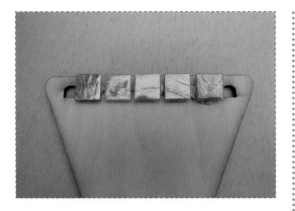

1)   Draw a line of glue across the top of the triangle, between the two holes. Place a beige tile in the centre, then add tiles to each side until you reach the holes.

2)   Now put a blob of glue in each top corner. Cut a beige tile in half diagonally to make two triangles. Place them so that the right angle of the triangle forms the top edge of the bunting.

3)   Working down the shape row by row, the next is made up of mirror tiles. Cut three mirror tiles into quarters. Add a line of glue beneath the beige tiles. Start in the middle, placing one mirror quarter in the centre. Working outward, place a tile at each side until you reach the edge.

4)   Cut the pink glitter tiles into long quarters. Apply another line of glue. Again start in the middle, but this time place two tiles so that the gap in between them is central. Place another tile on each side. You will be left with a gap at each side. To fill the gaps, trim a glitter long quarter to fit, ensuring to angle it slightly at the end so it fits the shape.

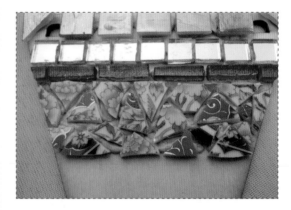

5)   A thick stripe of china sits beneath. Cut your china into small triangles roughly the same size and 1–1.5 cm (³⁄₈–⁵⁄₈ in) across. Apply a band of glue

to the wood, 3 cm (1¼ in) deep. Start at the centre top of the area, stick on the triangles so that a straight edge of china meets the straight edge of the glitter tiles. Now make a similar line at the bottom of the stripe. Fill in the gaps with more broken china pieces, cutting them to fit if necessary.

6)   Next place a row of whole pink iridescent tiles, placing the central tile first. To complete the row, you will need to make slanted cuts in the tiles.

7)   Add a row of glitter tile 8ths beneath, then a row of mirror tiles quarters, followed by a row of beige tile halves.

8)   Now working from the point of the heart upward, you will need one mirror tile 8th, one pink glitter tile 8th, one pink iridescent tile and some small pieces of china. Take the pink iridescent tile and cut off a corner. This will form the point at the bottom of the bunting. Stick it into place. Above this, stick the pink glitter tile, followed by the mirror tile. The space left is to be filled with china. Using the same method as before, fill in a stripe of china. Now set the bunting aside to dry.

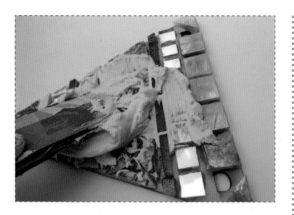

9) Grout the heart. Don't worry about covering the holes. Broken pottery may be slightly thicker than mosaic tiles, so the excess grout will need to be removed before it dries. Use your bare finger to do this, or wrap it in a piece of soft damp shammy leather. Set aside to dry then use a 'cross-head' screwdriver to gently screw through the grout to make the holes appear.

Tea-Light Holder

I've made these tea-light holders for weddings – they are so pretty when lit that they're the perfect evening decoration. They are such a simple design and can be made to match any colour scheme. In this project the mosaic tiles are stuck directly onto glass.

Transparent glass tiles are used, to allow the light from the candle to shine through the design.

You will need

5 mirror tiles

5 turquoise glitter tiles

5 blue opaque tiles

15 light blue iridescent tiles

15 dark blue iridescent tiles

20 blue transparent tiles

A glass tumbler. Anything cylindrical, clear and made from smooth glass will work, approximately 10 cm (4 in) diameter x 9 cm (3½ in) tall.

1) All the tiles in this project are cut into lengths. I like to get all of the cutting out of the way first. Cut the iridescent tiles into thirds lengthwise. Cut the rest of the tiles into long quarters.

2) Apply a straight line of glue from the top to the base of the glass. This needs to be fairly thick as you want the glue to 'grab' your tiles and hold them in place.

3) Place a first row of tiles onto the glass. I have started with a row of glitter tiles. We will be following a pattern with this design, and in-between each line of solid colour is a line of transparent tiles. Next add a line of transparent tiles to your glass. The pattern is:

Glitter

Transparent

Dark blue iridescent

Transparent

Blue opaque

Transparent

Light blue iridescent

Transparent

Mirror

Transparent

Once the glass is covered, set it aside to dry.

4)   I find the best way to grout glasses is to turn them upside down, place one hand inside and use this hand to turn the glass as I grout it. Remember to push the grout sideways as well as lengthways. Once you have grouted all the way around the tea-light, make sure to grout the top and bottom. Push the grout down over the edge of the glass and wipe away the excess as you go. Don't worry if the glass gets messy inside, this can be cleaned later. Wipe off the excess grout, following the line of the tiles. Wipe around the top to give a smooth surface. Any rough bits can be sanded once the grout is dry.

5)   Clean and polish the tea-light.

Garden Pot

With a dash of glitter and a flash of mirror, this pot is in danger of outshining the blooms it contains. Not only that, it's also quick to make, will last longer than your plants and will add a glimmer of sparkle to your garden. Ceramic pots can be bought in so many different places, from garden centres to charity shops, in all shapes and sizes. Try and find one that has a matt surface rather than a glossy one, as this will grip your tiles better.

You will need

15 mirror tiles

18 pink or purple glitter tiles

40 purple mix opaque tiles

20 purple opaque tiles

A garden pot. The one I have used for this project is approximately 10 cm (4 in) tall, 9 cm (3½ in) wide at the base, graduating up to 12 cm (5 in) wide at the top. This design will work with any size of pot. However, you may need more, or less, tiles.

1)   Start by defining the top of the pot with a colourful line of tiles. Cut all the glitter tiles and mirror tiles into quarters. Take around 20 of your purple mix and purple opaque (a mixture of all the hues) tiles and cut them into quarters too. Apply a 10 cm (4 in) line of glue around the top edge of your pot. This will allow you to work in stages.

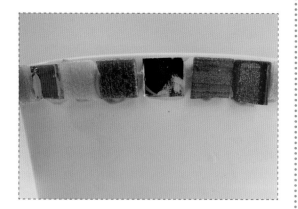

2)   Apply the quarter tiles around the top of the pot, making sure that the tops of the tiles are in line with the top of the pot. Place the rounded edges of the tiles so that they are along the top, to prevent sharp edges. Place your tiles in a random pattern.

3)   Repeat Step 2 so that you have two lines of quarters running around the pot. Avoid placing tiles of the same colour next to each other.

4)   Turn the pot upside down and repeat the last steps at the lower edge of the pot. Make sure that none of the tiles stick out below the base, to ensure that it sits flat when it is finished.

5)   Cut the remaining purple tiles (purple mix and purple) in half diagonally, into triangles. Apply triangles beneath the top border, so that the cut edge is against the bottom edge of quarter tiles. Continue

around the pot, alternating the hues of purple to achieve a good spread.

6) Place another row of triangles all the way around the pot, filling in the triangular gaps left by the top row.

7) Beneath the triangles add another line of quarter tiles, this time just using the glitter tiles and mirror tiles, alternating the colours as you go.

8) Add another row of triangles. Again, the cut edge should meet the row of quarter tiles. Remember to alternate the colours as you go.

9) Move to the bottom of the pot. Add a line of triangles, so that the cut edge is adjacent to the lower border tiles. You should be left with an 'open teeth' effect once you're finished.

10) Fill in the remaining space with tiles. Arrange these randomly within the gaps, remembering to keep spacing out the colours. You may need to cut some tiles into half again to fill in any small gaps. Once you have filled all of the space, set the pot aside to dry.

11) Grout the pot as for the tea-light and set aside to dry. Buff and polish.

Sun Circle House Number

Make a house number for your home using glitter tiles, mirror, bright opaques and an old-fashioned china plate. I have designed this project to be particularly versatile, so that you can alter the number as appropriate. If you have a very long house number, simply lengthen your MDF board and add more circles.

You will need

Sun templates

Broken china of your choice

25 iridescent blue tiles

20 iridescent black tiles

5 mirror tiles

5 gold glitter tiles

2 orange opaque tiles

3 yellow opaque tiles

A piece of medium density fibreboard (MDF) 21 x 17 cm (8¼ x 6¾ in) x 1 cm (³⁄₈ in) thick. This size is for a house number that is two numbers long; you will need a wider board if your house number is longer.

1) Draw your house number onto the MDF rectangle, leaving room for the border, and space to create the circular design somewhere on the sign. Decide where you would like the circles to be. If you have a 3, 5, 6, 8 or 9 in your house number, consider placing one of the circles inside the number. Don't worry if some of your 'suns' overlap your numbers.

2) The numbers are tiled first. They are the most important part of the design, and they need to be clearly legible. Cut the black tiles in half. Draw a thin line of glue over the house number, and apply the tiles. You may need to cut some of them at angles to make the numbers the right shape.

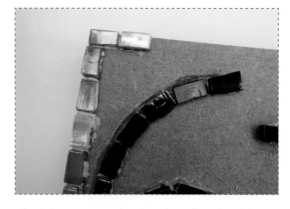

3) Move on to the border. Cut the blue tiles in half. Start in one corner, placing two tiles at right angles to each other. Work your way around the border. If you have drawn one of your circles on the edge of the board, it is a nice touch to create a break in the border around it. Cut your blue border tiles at angles to allow for this.

4) The circular 'suns' are made up of tiles cut into 16ths. Cut the gold, mirror, yellow and orange tiles into quarters. Then cut each quarter into quarters. Apply a line of glue around the edge of the circle and stick the gold 16ths in place. Repeat for all circles.

5) Apply a circle of mirror tiles inside your glitter tiles. Repeat for all 'suns'. Complete the small circle by filling in the centre with yellow tiles. In the medium circle, place a ring of yellow tiles, followed by orange tiles to fill the middle. The larger circle has room for a ring of yellow, followed by a ring of mirror, then orange, with a centre of yellow. When you fill in the centres you may want to cut a few of your tiny 16ths so that they fit in better.

6) Now fill in the rest of the design with broken china. Smash the pottery so that it is in relatively small pieces, then trim each with tile cutters so that you have a mix of shapes and sizes no larger than 3 cm (1¼ in) across. Start by placing the pieces around the border, lining up straight edges along the blue tiles.

7) Fill in the rest of the board placing the large pieces first, then when you can't fit any more in, trim the pieces to fit the specific shapes you have left. Try not to leave gaps wider than 2–3 mm (⅛ in). Set aside to dry overnight.

8) Grout the design. The pottery will have made the surface slightly uneven, and there will be depth differences to consider between the tiles and the china.

9) Cover your design in grout, including the edges. Once it is covered, and while wet, wipe around the whole design with your finger or small grout spatula. Be sure to wipe clear around all the circles and numbers. Set aside to dry.

10) Polish the design. To hang the sign, apply two ringed hooks (or similar) to the rear, and string with a strong wire or chain. Consider painting around the edge in a bright yellow, gold or blue to really set off your design. Make sure you use a wood paint suitable for outdoor use.

73

Bird-Shaped Jewel Box

Made using broken china, and recycled costume jewellery, this pretty birdy box ticks all of the boxes! I have incorporated parts of an old necklace that had leaf-shaped pendants on it, which are ideal for wings. It looks so pretty on a dressing table and is perfect for storing all those tricky bits and pieces that often get lost. Use bright paint inside and outside of your box for a finishing touch.

To keep the design light and delicate, I have added tiles to the top of the lid only. This allows you to add more decorative details around the side if you wish.

You will need

A papier-mâché box in the shape of a bird

Costume jewellery beads, for the eye detail

Gold and white 'leaves', for the wings (or a suitable alternative)

Broken china

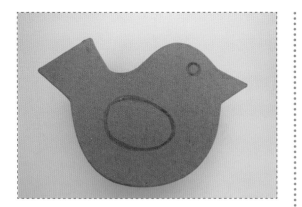

1) Draw the eye and wing detail on the bird. A small circle will suffice for the eye, and an egg or oval shape for the wing. Leave at least 1–2 cm (^{3}/$_8$–^{3}/$_4$ in) border around the wing.

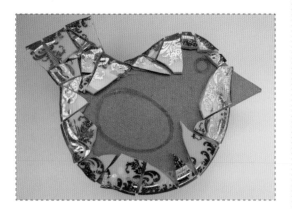

2) Trim the broken china pieces to a suitable size. Apply a thick line of glue to the bottom outer edge of the box lid. Use the edges of the pottery to form the edge

of the lid. Continue around the edge of the box.

3) Now fill in the body of your bird, leaving the eye and wing spaces free. Do not worry about cutting your tiles to fit perfectly around the eye and wing, as the jewellery will cover the edges of the tiles here. Set aside to dry.

4) Grout the lid of the box (if you attempted to grout around the jewellery, the grout would get into all the little details and be impossible to get out), covering the eye area completely and leave the wing area as clear as possible. Wipe off the excess grout and, with your finger, press some of the grout away from the eye hole, so that you are left with an indent. This way, the eye bead has room to 'sit in' its socket. Let the grout dry overnight.

5) Clean the lid with a grout sponge. Select the beads for the eye and wing details. Using the glue you would use to apply tiles to glass, apply a blob of glue to the eye area. Choose one large bead for the eye, or set smaller beads in a circle.

6) Apply the wing. Starting at the tip of the wing, apply a large thick blob of glue. Now place your chosen beads in a flat fan shape, keeping in mind the way a bird's feathers would fan out. Stick in place so that the ends are stuck well into the glue and the tips are 'feathered' out over the pottery. Apply more glue on top, so that it covers the base of the beads already applied. Add another layer of wings. Keep doing this until your wing shape is covered.

7) You may like to apply a few smaller beads at the front of the wing to finish off the design.

Tip: *If you find that you have any grout around the sides of your lid, or underneath, just sand it down with sandpaper until it is smooth again. Once you have a nice smooth surface you can paint it a complementary colour.*

Circular Jewel Box

Unlike the bird jewel box, this container is tiled both on top and on the sides. This gives it a really lovely reflective surface. The addition of some glamorous beads on top help finish the design with style. This would make a delightful accessory for a modern bedroom furnished with mirrored units, or look just as well in a shabby chic boudoir, adding a light-reflecting touch of sparkle.

You will need

Papier mâché circular craft box, 12 cm (4¾ in) diameter x 7 cm (2¾ in) deep

Costume jewellery

50 mirror tiles

15 turquoise glitter tiles

1) Gather together old and unwanted costume jewellery in complementary shades and designs. Separate the beads and charms so that they are ready for placing later.

2) Cut the mirror tiles into long quarters. Now apply two thin lines of glue on the side of the box lid.

3) Arrange the mirror tiles on the glue lines so that they are parallel to each other and vertical. The bottom of the tiles should be about 1 mm from the base of the lid. Continue all the way around the lid.

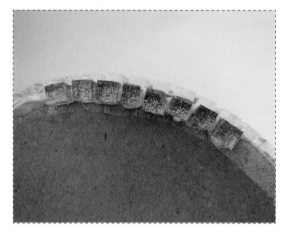

4) Put 10 glitter tiles aside for later use. Cut up the rest into 16ths. First cut each tile into quarters and then cut each quarter square into quarter squares. Apply a thin line of glue to the edge of the box lid. Apply the tiles a small section at a time, otherwise the glue will dry before you have finished adding tiles.

4) Draw two thin lines of glue, inside the border. Place one mirror tile on the glue lengthwise. Continue around the edge, ensuring the tiles are evenly fanned out.

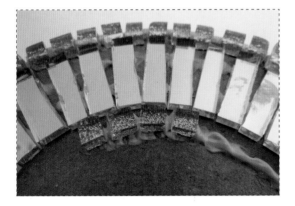

5) Form another circle inside the mirror tiles using glitter 16ths. Then place a circle of mirror tiles inside this.

6) Move on to the base of the box. Place the lid onto the base and press it down fully. Draw a line around the lip of the lid, where it meets the side of the box. Ensure all tiles are placed below this line, otherwise the box won't close.

7) Apply two thin lines of glue around the box. Place the mirror tiles vertically around the box and at least 3 mm ($^{1}/_{8}$ in) under the lid line. This leaves room for grout.

8) Add a bright line of glitter tiles around the base. Cut the remaining whole glitter tiles into quarter squares and stick them in a stripe around the base of the box. Leave the glue to dry overnight.

9) When you grout the box, leave the centre of the lid as clear of grout as possible. Grout the lid and base separately, wipe off the excess grout and allow each to dry. Clean and polish the box. Sand any excess grout from the inside of the lid, and the upper part of the base. This should allow the lid to slide on and off smoothly.

10) On the box lid, apply a circular base of beads for the decorative beads to sit on. This base helps to cover up the box. Apply a thick line of glue just inside the inner mirror circle. If you have a dangly bead or detail that you'd like to add to the box, then place it across the glue so that the beads hang out over the lid. Now apply a circle of your chosen beads. Save the best ones for the top and use plainer ones here. Do the same again so that you have two rings of beads and the box is mostly covered.

11) If you have any large beads, apply them first to the centre of your design. Keep adding beads and building up the design so that they look like a beautiful pile of jewels on top of the box. Fill in with the smaller beads. Finally add any embellishments. Leave to dry.

Christmas Bauble

Christmas is the ideal time to display your mosaic creations. Festive decorations celebrate everything gaudy and luxurious, and a room full of fairy lights will make your glass beauties shine to their fullest. When thinking about the design of these baubles, I decided that I wanted to stray away from the traditional Christmas colours and embrace a more modern festive feel.

I used a lovely plate I found that features bright pinks, greens, yellows and blues. To accompany its vibrant patterns I have used some glitter tiles and mirror. This will be softened by some beige iridescents. I hope you agree that this Christmas bauble is both funky and festive.

You will need

Polystyrene (styrofoam) sphere 7 cm (2¾ in) diameter (any bigger and your bauble will be very heavy)

Bauble pin or screw eye hook

Broken china with your choice of pattern

9 pink glitter tiles

3 turquoise glitter tiles

4 mirror tiles

25 beige iridescent tiles

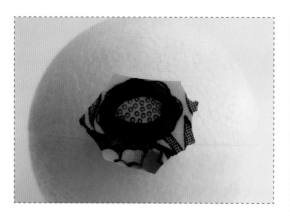

1) We are going to be using a star shape as the central design on our bauble. For the centre of the star, from broken pottery, choose a small-scale motif and cut it out so that you have a rough round tile, approximately 1.5 cm (⅝ in) across. The top of the polystyrene ball has a little circle on it. Keep this at the top of the design as you work. Imagine that the sphere is a globe, and place the circle somewhere along the equator.

2) Now cut five rough triangles from the same pottery, about 1 cm (⅜ in) wide at the base and 1.5 cm (⅝ in) long.

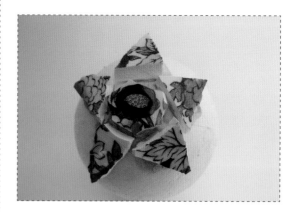

3) Place the first triangle along one edge of the circle tile, so that its tip points away from the circle. Place the rest of the triangles around the circle to form a star shape.

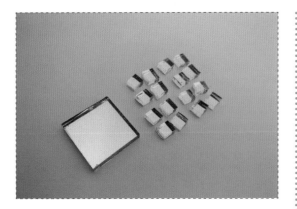

4) To make a border around the star using mirror tile, cut each mirror tile into 16ths.

6) Cut the turquoise glitter tiles into 16ths. Repeat Step 3 to apply them all the way around the edge of the star.

5) Apply a line of glue along one edge of the star. Place a mirror tile at the tip of the star and one more close to the centre. Now fill between these two tiles with more mirror tiles, trimming a tile to fit if necessary. Repeat around the star.

7) To make a circle around the star, set aside three pink glitter tiles for later and cut the rest into 16ths. Apply a line of glue between two points of the star, following the curve of the sphere as you apply it so that it has a rounded appearance. Start at the tip of the star and apply a line of your pink glitter 16ths along the line. Continue until you have a pink circle around the star. Avoid the area where your hanging hook will be. Your pink line should be a couple of millimetres in front of the top of your ball.

8)   Next, fill the blank areas inside the circle with beige tiles. Cut all the beige tiles into quarter squares. Work on one space at a time and start by covering the area in glue. Fit as many whole quarters as you can along the line of the pink glitter circle. You will probably have to cut a tile in half to fill this space. Cut some triangles to fill the remaining space. Fill all the space within your circle using the same method.

9)   Complete the first half by applying two rings of beige quarter square tiles. Start at the top of the bauble, where the hook will be placed. Leave at least a 1 cm (³/₈ in) square space for the hook.

10)   Take the glitter tiles you set aside earlier and cut them into 8ths. Apply a line of glue around the bauble and place the tiles to form a circle, along the edge of the neutral tiles.

11)   Fill the remaining space with broken china. Cut up the china into rough triangles, all smaller than 1 cm (³/₈ in). Apply a thick band of glue, leaving a circle of around 2.5–3 cm (1–1 ¼ in) clear in the middle. Apply the triangles so that their straight edges line up with the pink glitter tiles. You should end up with a circle of triangles pointing inward. Now take some more china triangles and place them so they fill in the gaps between the points, and add more until you have a thick circular band, with a rough circle clear in the middle.

12) Fill in the rest of the bauble. Use a circle of pink glitter tiles, and fill in the centre with mirror tiles. You will have to cut the mirror tiles randomly to fill the centre circle. Once you have completed the tiling stage, set your bauble aside to dry.

13) Screw in the eye hook at the top by applying gentle pressure as you twist the hook into position.

14) Grout the bauble starting around the hook area, pushing the grout over and inwards around the base of the hook. This will ensure a good strong hold once it is dry. DO NOT hold or move the hook while you are grouting, as you risk dislodging it from the polystyrene. Wipe off the excess grout once you've finished, ensuring that you pay special attention to the china areas. Set aside to dry.

15) Clean and polish the bauble. Add a ribbon of your choice and it is ready for the tree!.

Christmas Tree

This design involves many different techniques and lots of cuts. It's an ideal project to complete in small sections, as the last stage of 'filling in' is meticulous and lengthy, though I hope you agree that it's well worth the effort. Adorned with beautiful beads and glinting with mirror and iridescent tiles, this tree is the height of Christmas luxury. It will look great on your festive table, mantelpiece, or anywhere that it can reflect those twinkling Christmas lights.

You will need

Cardboard (card stock), papier mâché or polystyrene (styrofoam) cone, 20 cm (8 in) tall

An assortment of jewellery beads for baubles, 0.5–1 cm (¼–½ in)

A large bead for the top of the tree

4 mirror tiles

5 beige iridescent tiles

3 purple glitter tiles

60 green iridescent tiles

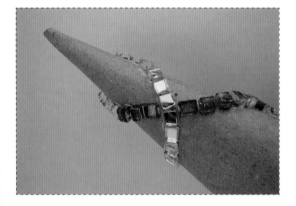

1) Draw directly onto the cardboard cone. Start with a line that wraps around the tree, as if you are drawing on a length of ribbon or tinsel.

2) Cut the mirror tiles into 16ths. Apply a thin line of glue starting from the top of your tree and apply the mirror 16ths along it. Do this in small sections and work your way down to the base.

3) Draw a second line curling around the tree from the top to the base. Make the lines cross in a couple of places. Cut the glitter tiles into 16ths. Apply a line of glue and place the tiles neatly along the line.

4) Draw another line from the top to the base and cover with neutral iridescent tiles cut into 8ths. Place them lengthways along your line of glue.

5)   Cut the black tiles into 16ths. They will add a lovely intricacy and delicacy to your finished tree. Draw circles at intervals around the tree. Make the circles slightly wider than your beads. Now, apply a ring of glue to each circle and arrange the black 16ths around it.

6)   Fill in the rest of the tree with dark green iridescent tiles. Take your time. If you work in stages with long gaps between tiling, make sure you wipe away any excess glue at the end of each tiling session. Cut the green tiles into quarters. Start gluing the whole quarters onto the blank spaces, starting at the base and positioning them so that the squares are aligned. Alternatively place the green quarters 'randomly', filling in the spaces without cutting to fit each shape exactly.

7) Place the green quarters all the way up the tree. Either place all the whole quarters that you can and then start filling in all the gaps, or fill in the gaps as you go.

8) Once you reach the top of the tree, cut the quarters in half. This is because the tip is thinner and will look bulky if you try and stick quarters on it. The largest bead will sit on top of the tree so it helps if the tree tip has a flat top.

9) Grout the tree. Place a hand inside the tree and use this to rotate it as you grout. Take special care when wiping off the excess. Follow the lines of the 'tinsel' and wipe separately around each bauble. Also, press your little finger gently into each bauble circle to create a slight dent. Set aside to dry.

10) Take a small screwdriver and gently scrape out the space where each bead will go. Do this as deep as you can without removing all of the grout – a depth of 1 mm will make a difference.

11) Select a pile of beads that are roughly the right size for your baubles. Use glue that is recommended for use on glass and ensure that it dries clear. Apply a

blob of glue to each hole and stick on the beads.

12) Choose a larger bead for the tip of the tree. Add a large blob of glue and place your bead on top. You may need to hold it in place for a minute or two to ensure that it sits straight.

Owl Lantern

The popularity of the owl as a design image has never been stronger, and I have chosen to embrace this with my lantern design. One of the best uses for empty food jars is to turn them into lanterns. I have designed my cute owly face using glitter tiles, iridescents and transparents. The importance of transparent tiles is obvious when making a lantern, and therefore they feature heavily in this project.

You will need

Owl templates

A glass jar, 10 cm (4 in) diameter x 12 cm (5¾ in) tall.

1 orange opaque tile

2 black flat rounds (or rounded pebbles if you prefer), 2 cm (¾ in)

4 mirror tiles

3 dark green transparent tiles

3 light green transparent tiles

4 gold glitter tiles

14 beige iridescent tiles

25 dark blue transparent tiles

10 light blue transparent tiles

Wire, for hanging

1) Ensure that the glass jar is clean and grease-free. Place the owl eye templates on the jar and stick in place. Place them 5 mm (¼ in) apart and roughly 2 cm (¾ in) below the neck of the jar. Draw around them with a permanent marker.

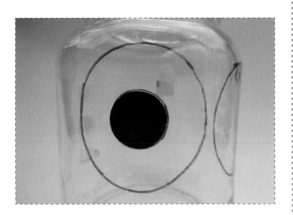

2) Using transparent glue suitable for glass on glass projects, place the black rounds for the owl's pupils. Put a blob of glue in the centre of each circle and press the rounds on firmly.

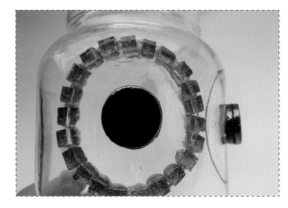

3) Stick a ring of gold tile 16ths around the outer edge of the eyes. Try and keep the edges of the tiles in line in a neat circle. Repeat for the other eye.

4) Cut the green (light and dark) transparent tiles into 8ths. Apply glue into the gap in the circle between the black pupil and the gold tiles. Alternate shades of green and fill the circle until the eye is complete. Do the same for the other eye.

5) Cut the orange tile in half diagonally to create two triangles. Place one triangle between the eyes, at the bottom, to form a beak.

6) Use the beige iridescent tiles to create the owl's ears and face. Take two whole beige tiles and stick them, with a large bob of glue, to the tops of each circle. Place them toward the outsides of the eyes, so that they look like pointy ears.

7) Cut two beige tiles in half diagonally. Place a triangle on each side of the owl's ears, so that the cut side aligns with the gold glitter tiles.

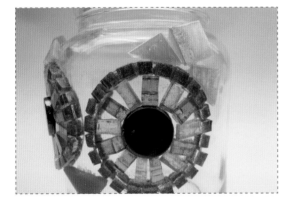

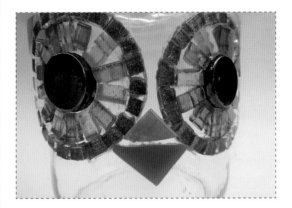

8) Cut another beige tile in half diagonally. Place one half above the orange 'beak' tile. If it is too large, trim it slightly to fit.

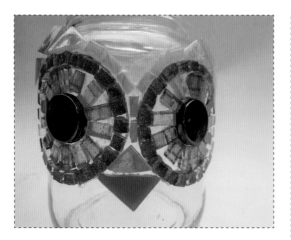

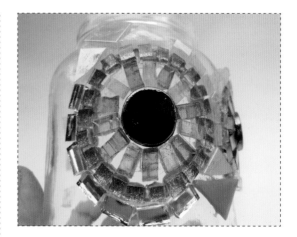

9) Cut another beige tile into 8ths. Place two of these above the triangle you just stuck on, so that they fill the gap between the eyes. If they are slightly too thick, either choose thinner ones or cut them down slightly. Place the remaining six tiles along the top of the eyes, starting inside the top triangles and coming downward toward the beak tile. You should have a tiny gap left. Take the triangle you had left in Step 8 and cut off one of its tips to form a tiny triangle. Place this in the gap.

10) Cut the mirror tiles into 8ths. Apply a line of glue from one side of the beak, around the eye and up to meet the neutral triangle tile. Stick the tiles along this line. If you are left with a gap smaller than your tiles, cut one down to size and pop it in. Do the same on the other side of the beak.

11) Add another line of mirror tiles, this time starting slightly below the top mirror tile of the first line. Keep applying tiles until you reach the second to last tile, closest to the beak. This will give your owl's feathery cheeks a nice gradation.

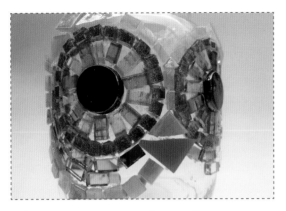

12) Cut the remaining beige tiles into quarters. Apply a line of glue from one side of the beak, all the way around the mirror tiles and up to meet the owl's ears. Apply neutral tiles in a line from the beak to the end of the mirror tiles. Once you reach the last mirror tile, place a beige quarter on top of it, so that the beige tiles meet up with the ears. Now do the same on the other side.

13) Take two beige quarters and cut them in half diagonally. Take two of the triangles and place them between the two quarters just placed. This should give a smooth outline to your owl's face. Repeat on the other side with your final two triangles.

14) Cut all the blue tiles (light and dark) into quarters. Apply a patch of glue to the empty 'v' shape above the owl's face. Place one dark blue tile between the eyes so that its corner is pointing downward to the beak. Place one on each side of this tile, corners facing downward. Then complete the triangle of blue tiles by placing your last three quarters across the top, corners down. Point the cut edges downward to prevent sharp corners at the top of your lantern. By twisting the quarters so that they appear to be a diamond shape, we create a really feathery effect.

15) Apply glue to the base of the owl's face, below the beak in a diamond shape. Still using only dark blue quarters, apply a tile underneath the beak so that its top corner meets the beak's bottom corner. Apply a tile on each side of this one so that the straight edges meet the straight edges of the neutral tiles. Now stick another tile underneath these three, in the centre, corner pointing down. If you are too close to the base of the jar to do this, just leave this bottom tile off. Add three tiles each side, around the base of the owl's face, so that the corners are pointing down and they create a zigzag effect. This gives the appearance of a feathery face!

16) Add a border of dark blue quarters all the way around each side until they meet the ears at the top of the face. These tiles should be placed in a line so that their flat edges meet the flat edges of the neutral tiles.

17) Complete the rest of the lantern using blue transparent tiles. Apply a thick line of glue all the way around the top of the jar. The curved top edge of the jar is clear of tiles. Starting with a line of dark blue quarters, place your first quarter squarely on the glass, so that its top edge is level with the base. Stick your tiles in a line from one edge of the owl's face to the other.

18) Add another line of glue underneath the tiles you just placed and apply a line of light blue quarters. Continue to alternate colours down the jar until you have covered it completely. Set the lantern aside to dry.

19) Grout the lantern taking care with the pointy feather details. Push the grout down into the top and bottom blue tiles, to ensure that it is fully surrounding them. When wiping, ensure that you leave enough grout below them to keep them secure, but try to remove any excess in-between them so that they don't lose their zigzag effect. Set aside to dry. Clean and polish the lantern.

20) Use part of an old metal hanger for the hook. You will need a slightly thinner wire for the anchors that will hold your hook in place. Thin jewellery wire or garden wire is perfect. Create a loop that is at least 4 cm (1½ in) wider in diameter than the neck of the jar. Seal the loop into a circle by wrapping the ends of the wire together. Place the circle of wire over the neck of your jar, and pull from each end so that the wire is tight underneath the thread. Now twist the wire on each side to create two hoops. Pop in two pencils and keep twisting until the loops are small. Toward the end, it may help to use some small pliers to twist the wire tightly. You should be left with strong small loops for your hook. Using pliers, bend your hanger wire into shape and hook onto the jar. I have wrapped green taffeta ribbon around the rim of my jar.

Floral Tray

The base of a tray is the perfect surface to mosaic, and if you don't use a tray then you can always hang it on a wall as a decorative item. Due to the revival of vintage style, trays are officially back in fashion. You can buy unfinished wooden trays online or in a charity shop or thrift stores.

I have provided a template for this design, which can be used on any size or shape of tray that you have sourced. If your tray is a different shape to mine, simply arrange the flowers wherever you want. Floral themes are always a favourite. If it's a small tray then one flower would look lovely on its own, perhaps with a couple of green leaves.

You will need

Floral tray templates

35 x 25 cm (13¾ x 10 in) raw/unfinished wooden tray

20 green iridescent tiles

24 purple glitter tiles

30 purple and purple mix opaque tiles

1 or 2 dinner plates of any pattern, in complementary colours

1) Cut out the large and small flower and leaf templates. Place the large flower on the tray, wherever you think looks pretty, and draw around it with a pencil. Find the exact centre of the flower. Mark it with a pencil, flip the template over and scribble quite hard on the other side to transfer the carbon to the tray.

2) Take a bright marker pen. Starting from the centre of the flower shape, curve a line outward to meet the top edge of the petals. Do this all the way around, until you have a similar shape to the illustration.

3) Place the smaller flowers and draw around them in pencil. Define each petal as before. Now, join the flowers together with a gently swooping line to represent the stem. Add a couple of leaves, drawing around your leaf templates. When you are happy with the design, draw over the stem and petals in marker pen to create a clear template for placing the tiles.

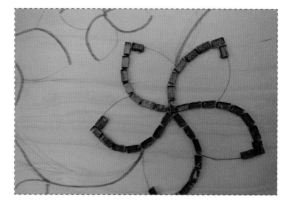

4) Cut the glitter tiles into 8ths for the outline of the petals. Apply the glue along the pen line. Always start by forming the tip of a petal by placing two tiles at an angle to each other. Continue applying tiles down the edge of the petal to the centre. Repeat this for all of the petals, ensuring you scrape away excess glue after each one.

5) Fill in the gaps to complete the petal outlines, making a diagonal cut to fit the last tile. Repeat the above steps for all the flowers, until you have finished the outlines.

6) For the stems, cut the green tiles in half. Place a line of glue along the stem and line the halves along it. The stem runs at the back of the flowers. Make sure that the rounded edges of the tiles are not all on the same side to give the stem a more even appearance. As you reach a flower, you may need to make a diagonal cut to fit the tiles.

7) Cut the green tiles in half. Create the leaf tip using a corner of a tile, then fill in the rest of the shape. Work around the outline first and then cut up the tiles, as needed, to fill the middle.

8) Fill in the petals. You will need roughly 30 purple tiles in an array of hues. Cut them into 8ths. I prefer to cut up all the tiles I need before I start, so that I can work quickly.

9) Working on one petal at a time, apply glue to the petal centre. Start at the tip, mirroring the outline, and apply a line of tiles. Add another line inside the first one, and continue until a small gap remains, then trim a tile to fit.

10) For this design I chose a pretty pattern of china to fill the background, using quite plain tones, as I wanted the bright flowers to be the focal point of the tray. As you are making a tray, it's important to choose relatively fine china. Smash the china, then take the flat pieces and cut them with tile nippers so that they are roughly the same size (no more than 4 cm (1½ in) and all different shapes.

11) Always start with the edges and draw a line of glue along the length of one edge. Place the straightest edges of the tiles along it. Repeat for all edges. Next, match up the pointy pieces of china with the triangular gaps around the petals.

12) Fill in the rest of the space. I usually start in one corner and work my way around until I've finished. Cut tiles to fit any gaps. If you prefer, you could start by sticking down as many tiles as you can, without making any cuts, and then start cutting to fill in the small gaps. Leave to dry overnight.

13) Grout the design, pushing the grout firmly into the corners to prevent holes. Wipe away any excess grout, paying close attention to the pottery pieces. Wipe as much grout as you can off the wood.

14) Clean and polish the mosaic. Sand the wood if you wish to paint the rest of the tray so that the paint grips and all excess grout is removed. Cover the mosaic with newspaper, using masking tape around the edges, to ensure all of the tiles are covered. Paint the wood with a brush or use spray paint (my favoured method) in your chosen colour.

3D Heart

Another heart project, but this time it's three-dimensional and because of its larger size, there's the opportunity to add some words to the design. Feel free to change the colours to suit your décor.

You will need

A 3D polystyrene (styrofoam) heart 12 x 12 cm (4¾ x 4¾ in)

1 hook screw eye

9 turquoise glitter tiles

14 mirror tiles

17 blue iridescent tiles

3 dark blue opaque tiles

2 light blue opaque tiles

Ribbon, for hanging

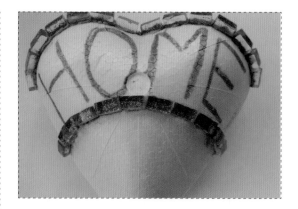

1) Write your choice of word across the front of the polystyrene heart. Use a permanent marker and space the letters out evenly, leaving at least 1.5 cm (5/8 in) border at each side of the word. Draw a gently curving line following the shape of the heart. Draw another line above.

2) Cut all of the glitter tiles into 8ths. Apply a line of glue along the line above the writing and starting at one end, apply the first tile at an angle, so that it points slightly upward toward the top of the heart. Keep placing tiles along the line, making sure that the last tile is angled like the first. You may need to adjust the tiles slightly once they're stuck on, to ensure that both sides are even. Complete the bottom line using the same method.

3) Take five of the iridescent blue tiles and cut them into 8ths. Apply a line of glue underneath the top line of glitter tiles and stick the tiles along the glue, following the shape of the glitter tiles. Do the same above the lower line of glitter tiles.

4) Apply glue over the first letter. Place the glitter tile 8ths on the shape, starting with any horizontal strokes. Fill the vertical lines cutting any tiles to fit, then any rounded letter parts. Repeat for all letters.

5) The lower half of the heart is filled with stripes. Start by cutting all of the mirror tiles into 8ths. Apply a line of 8ths beneath the lower line of glitter tiles. Cut the rest of the iridescent blue tiles into quarters. Place a line of these under the line of mirror tiles.

6) Cut the light blue opaque tiles into 8ths. Add a line of these underneath the iridescent tiles. Your line should be more like an arch now, as the tiles start to follow the shape of the heart.

7) Take six of the mirror 8ths and cut them in half. Apply these as the next line.

8) Add a row of opaque dark blue tiles cut into 8ths. Cut the remaining glitter tiles in half and apply the little squares to the point of the heart.

9) Next, using blue iridescent tiles, fill in the area around the letters, placing as many whole quarters as you can in the gap. After this you will need to cut them as you go.

10) Apply a line of mirror 8ths above the top line of glitter tiles. Then add an opaque dark blue line. The top of the heart will be filled with iridescent quarters. Cover the area in glue and add a line of tiles to each side, making sure to leave around 1.5 cm (5/8 in) space for the hook. Use triangular tiles at the ends of the rows. Fill in the top of the heart by cutting the quarters into 8ths and applying a line of them. Set aside to dry.

11) Once the first side is dry, fill in the other side of the heart. Apply the iridescent blue quarters all the way around the edge of the heart. Start at the bottom and place the first tile so that one of its corners becomes the tip of the heart. Make sure the rounded edge of the tile is facing outward. Continue all the way around to the beginning.

12) Place a line of mirror 8ths inside the blue tiles, starting at the bottom. Repeat the last two steps twice more.

13) To fill the central space, make a small rough heart shape, using blue iridescent quarters.

14) Fill in the rest of the space with mirror tiles. Set aside to dry completely.

15) Screw the hook into the heart using gentle pressure. Once the hook is in place, grout the heart, making sure you push it in and around the hook so that the bottom of it is completely covered. Pat the grout down slightly with your finger. Smooth down and wipe off any excess grout then leave the mosaic to dry.

16) Polish the heart. Add a ribbon to hang the heart.

Meadow in a Bowl

As soon as I saw this wooden bowl I knew that I had to create a fun, bright design for the inside. I decided on a floral theme, taking inspiration from the wild flower meadows I remember from my childhood. This design will fit all sizes of bowl. If you have a small bowl then simply use one of each flower. If your bowl is large then you can go mad and fill it with blooms!

You will need

1 wooden bowl

3 red glitter tiles, for the red tulip

1 red opaque tile, for the red tulip

1 red transparent tile, for the red tulip

3 yellow opaque tiles, for the yellow dandelion

1 orange opaque tile, for the yellow dandelion

2 green transparent tiles, for the yellow dandelion

4 purple opaque tiles, for the lavender

2 blue transparent tiles, for the blue bud

2 dark green transparent tiles, for the blue bud

Green and dark green iridescent tiles, for the stems

Blue iridescent tiles, for the bowl infill

119

1)   Cut out the flower templates provided. Arrange them in the bowl and stick in place temporarily. Draw around the shapes. Make sure that the flowers don't overlap and allow room for flower stems, which run from the base of the flowers to the centre of the bowl. Don't overlap the flowers and stems.

2)   For the tulip, cut the red glitter tiles into 8ths for the outline. Apply a line of glue onto the shape, around the bottom and up to the tip on one side. Stick the tiles along the glue line, starting from the bottom.

3)   Apply a line of glue down the other side of the petal, then stick a line of tiles along this line.

4)   Create a second petal behind the first, applying glue along the left side of the flower. Cut one of the 8ths into a triangle. Place it, pointing down, to fit to the bottom left of the tulip. Complete the line of glitter tiles, moving up to the tip of the flower. Create a point at the tip by adding a small triangle of tile between the left and right petals.

5) Fill the tulip using a mix of opaque and transparent reds cut into 8ths. Place them all vertically so that they follow the shape of the template. Repeat for any other tulips.

6) For the bud, cut the green transparent tiles into long quarters. Cut half of them in half again. Cover the bottom half of the bud with glue. Add a blob underneath the shape, in the centre. Place one of the 8ths on this blob for the top of the stem. Now place two long quarters above and to each side of this tile, pointing upward to create a 'V' shape. Use four 8ths to fill in between the 'V'.

7) Apply a line of glue across the bud, above the tiles. Add more green 8ths vertically along this line.

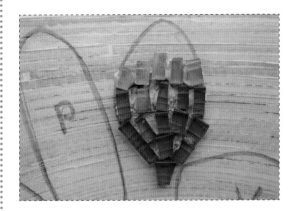

8) Cut the blue transparent tiles into 8ths. Apply glue across the bud. Add five blue tiles vertically, following the outline. Add another row of blue tiles on top, again tilting them inward. Fill all of the blue buds in this way.

9) For the lavender, cut the purple tiles into 8ths. Cover the bottom third of the lavender in glue. Cut one iridescent green tile into long quarters, and place two in a vertical line in the centre of the glue. Place two purple tiles on each side, as if creating wings.

10) Apply glue to the rest of the shape. Fill with purple tiles angled upward and sticking out at different angles. Complete any other lavender shapes in this manner.

11) For the dandelion, take two green transparent tiles. Cut one into long quarters and one into square quarters. Apply a line of glue to the base of the shape. Place one square quarter at the bottom in the centre, and turned en pointe. Put one long quarter on each side, defining the shape of the dandelion. Next, take two more long quarters and place them in-between the tiles you have just

stuck on, creating a forked shape with four prongs.

12) Cut the orange tile into 8ths. Place these between the green tiles.

13) Cut the yellow tiles into 8ths. These will form the rest of the dandelion petals.

Dandelions are wild and straggly. Try and re-create this with your tiles.

14) Fill all the flower shapes.

15) For the stems, it looks great if you continue the stem using the same green tiles that you used in the flower. Cut the green tiles as you go and continue the stems down into the centre of the bowl.

16) Create an iridescent green circle in the centre of the bowl, using tiles cut into quarters. Work from the middle, and apply the tiles in circles, outward until the circle meets all the stems.

17) For the infill, cut the iridescent blue tiles into quarters. I cut 20 tiles at a time. Apply a line of glue around the top of the bowl, then a line of tiles on top, ensuring that the rounded edges are facing up and level with the top of the bowl. Keep filling until the bowl is complete. Once you have filled all the gaps, set aside to dry. When grouting, push the grout in all directions to ensure that it fills all of the holes. Grout into the top edge of the bowl to create a smooth edge. Wipe around the edge after grouting to remove excess grout.

Peacock Vase

This peacock vase is quite a technically challenging piece. I have used iridescent tiles, glitter tiles and transparent tiles in this beautiful project, all in the different hues of a peacock's feathers. You can also use this vase as a stunning light fixture; simply pop a candle, or a string of battery operated fairy lights inside!

I have provided a template for this design, as the peacock feather will form the centre of your vase. The vase I have used for this project is a circular 'bowl'-shaped glass vase, although this design would work well with any shape as long as one of the sides is wide enough to fit the template.

You will need

Peacock template

Glass vase

One black glass pebble, approximately 2 cm (¾ in), for the feather design

15 black iridescent tiles, for the feather design

8 beige iridescent tiles, for the feather design

1 blue opaque tile, for the feather design

5 turquoise glitter tiles, for the feather design

6 green iridescent tiles, for the feather design

12 blue transparent tiles, for the feather design

Mirror tiles, for the vase infill

Black iridescent tiles, for the vase infill

Blue transparent tiles, for the vase infill

1) Cut out the templates provided. Arrange the templates on the vase in a central position using sticky tac. Allow 3 cm (1 ¼ in) from the top of your template to the top of the vase. Roughly draw around each template with a permanent marker. If you are using a circular vase, wrap the template around the vase gently as you draw around it.

2) Using glue suitable to stick glass on glass, apply a blob directly onto the centre of the feather. Place the glass pebble just above the upside down 'V'.

3) Cut one black iridescent tile in half diagonally. Stick the two triangles underneath the pebble, in a line.

4) Cut the opaque blue tile in 16ths and arrange them around the rest of the pebble. If the tile has a bevelled edge and is tricky to keep flat, then try placing it against the pebble.

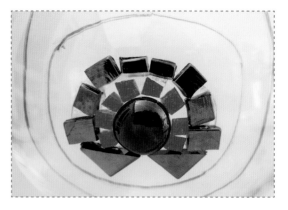

5) Cut two black iridescent squares in half. Cut two of the halves into quarters. Cut roughly a third off each remaining half. Arrange them around the blue tiles, with the two smallest lying horizontal across the top.

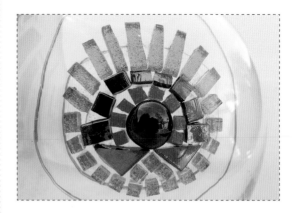

6) Cut three glitter tiles into long quarters. Place four lengths fanned around the centre top of the feather. Trim six of the rest, arranging them so that the height decreases slightly as you place them around the circle. Cut the remaining glitter tiles into 16ths, and use these to form the rest of the oval.

7) Cut three iridescent green tiles into quarters. These 12 quarters make up the top of the next oval. Cut two more green tiles into 8ths. These will make up the bottom of the oval shape. Arrange them so that the outline is smooth.

8) Cut three beige iridescent tiles in half. Discard one half for now. Place the five halves at the top of the oval. Cut one more beige tile in half and one into

quarters. Cut roughly 1–2 mm off the top of each half. Place on each side of the five already on the vase. Arrange the quarters equally on each side of these. The rest of the oval is made up of 8ths.

9) The next oval is made up of black iridescent tiles. Cut three into quarters. Cut another four into 8ths. Arrange them on the vase with the large quarters at the top and the smaller 8ths around the bottom.

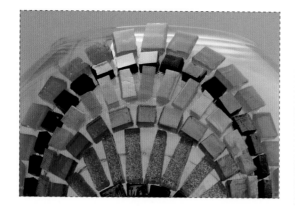

10) Cut three transparent blue tiles in half. These form a line from the top of the feather to the base of the vase. Centre one half above the oval, meeting the top of the vase. Place the rest in a vertical line from the middle of the bottom of the oval, to the base of the vase.

11) Cut another blue tile in half. Trim 1–2 mm off each and place these to each side of the top blue tile. Cut two more blue tiles into quarters. Place four quarters on each side of the middle tiles, following the curve of the oval. The rest of the oval is made up of 8ths. You will need four tiles, cut into 8ths, to complete the oval. Once the oval is complete, use

those spare 8ths to make up the design at the bottom of the feather. The peaccok feather is now complete.

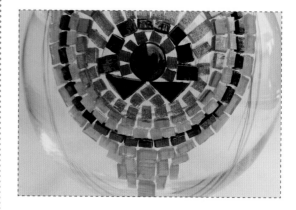

12) Draw a line down each side of the peacock feather, roughly 5 mm (¼ in) from the edge of the feather design on each side.

13) You will needs lots of mirror tiles to complete the vase. Cut 20 at a time into long quarters. Apply glue along the pen line. Place the mirror tiles along the line, and then adjust them so that they are straight. Do this on both sides.

14) Now fill around the feather design with mirror tiles. Start above the feather. Apply

glue liberally to the area and work on one section at a time. Place a quarter length next to the border line. You may need to make diagonal snips to the tiles to fill in the rest of the space. Repeat on the other side.

15) Now fill below the peacock feather. Apply 'whole' lengths first then clip any tiles that require diagonal cuts to fill smaller spaces. Make sure that the tiles align horizontally and vertically, for a really neat finish.

16) Fill in the rest of your vase. I have chosen to use vertical stripes of blue transparent, black iridescent and mirror tiles. The transparent tiles help the vase to glow if you put lights inside it. Therefore it is essential that they feature all the way around the vase. Cut another 20 or so mirror tiles into long quarters. Cut the same amount of black and blue tiles and cut them all in half.

17) Work on each side of the vase in turn, to ensure that the design is even. Apply a line of glue down the left side of the mirror tiles. Add a line of mirror tiles. Repeat on the other side.

18) Follow this with a line of black tiles, then another line of mirror, then the blue tiles. Repeat this pattern, adding a line each side, until you have covered the front of your vase.

19) If you have a circular vase, you will find that the lines become more curved until they meet up to form an oval at the back. If this is the case, then complete the oval neatly and apply vertical stripes inside it.

20) If your vase is cylindrical or square, you should be able to add stripes all the way around. Set the piece aside to dry.

21) This is a large project to grout and will be heavy. Start to apply grout to the most intricate area – the feather oval. Work the grout in all directions and wipe off the excess, following the path of the tiles with your fingers. Continue until the whole vase is complete. Leave to dry then scrub with a grouting sponge to remove excess grout, and then polish it.

Gaudi-Inspired Clock

This final design is inspired by the king of mosaic, Antoni Gaudi. I wanted this clock to remind me of the wonderful ceiling details he created in the 'Chamber of the Hundred Columns' in Park Güell, Barcelona. They are full of sweeping shapes, bright colours and broken china! It is said that he used broken plates from his own house, glass bottles and even broken china dolls in his mosaics.

You will need

A circle of medium density fibreboard (MDF) 50 cm (19¾ in) diameter and no more than 1.5 cm (⅝ in) thick)

Drill, to make a hole in the centre of your wood

Clock hands and movement – 23 cm (9⅛ in) with French spade hands (black)

Broken china in a variety of designs

30 gold glitter and yellow opaque tiles

40 orange-gold glitter and orange iridescent tiles

30 purple opaque, purple mix and purple glitter tiles

60 mirror tiles

30 turquoise glitter and blue transparent tiles

30 red glitter and red transparent tiles

40 light green iridescent tiles

30 pink glitter tiles

1) Draw a line across the middle of the circle, through the centre point. Draw a second line dividing the circle into quarters. Measure the circumference of the circle and divide each quarter into three equal measurements. Mark these measurements around the edge of the circle. Join up the marks until you have 12 equal sections.

2) To create curved sections on the clock face, use the edge of a large plate, or similar flat circular object. Line up the plate so that it touches the centre point, and the top of one of the sections. Draw around the edge of the plate. Repeat all the way around the clock.

3) Refer to the instructions on the clock kit for the size of the hole required to thread the arm mechanism through. Drill a hole to the required size.

4) I have designed this clock so that it has two stripes of china tiles and two stripes of mirror. The rest of the sections are made up of blocks of colour, each one different. Arrange the tile colours on the clock front before you start in order to help you decide what colour goes where. It looks great if the mirror sections appear opposite each other. I have done the same with the broken china. Mark your choice of tile in each section.

5) Starting with the first tile section, cut the tiles into long quarters. Start in the centre of the clock and avoid placing a tile over the hole. Apply a line of glue from the centre of the circle to the edge, along the inside edge of a wavy line. Place a long quarter on the glue line at the centre of the clock. Now place a long quarter at the edge of the design, along the glue line so that there is a full tile at each end. Complete the line of mirror tiles.

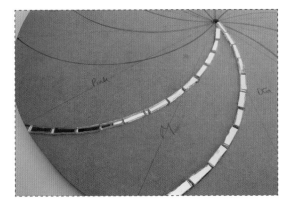

6) Now draw a line of glue along the other edge of the same section. Keep the glue just inside the line. Place a long quarter at the edge. Take another long quarter and cut one of its ends so that it is pointed, and fits in next to the central tile. Complete the line with more long quarters.

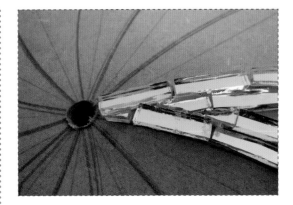

7) Work inward, apply a line of tiles inside each tiled line until the section is filled. Cut the tiles closest to the centre at angles to fit them in. Make sure that you use whole long quarters, at the edges and spread them evenly. Always start the lines by applying a tile to each end first, before completing the line.

8) Move onto the next section. Use the same method as for the first section.

9) For the green section, use a mix of transparent and iridescent tiles cut into long quarters. Cut the iridescent tiles into thirds, as they are smaller. This should give you tiles of a similar width to work with. Apply the tiles as before interspersing iridescent tiles and transparent tiles evenly throughout the sections.

10) For the broken china section, I have chosen a couple of different types of china, featuring toning colours. Cut up the china into different shapes and sizes. As you are working on a large piece, you can have a wide range of sizes. For the china sections, place pieces all around the edge

first, before filling in the middle. Place a pointy tile in the centre of the design.

11) Apply a thick line of glue all the way along one side of the section. Place a piece of china at the end of the glue, at the edge of the circle. Choose a piece that fits nicely into the triangular shape, or cut one to fit. Complete the row of tiles, making sure that you place flat edges of tile straight along the edge of your section. Repeat this all the way around the edge.

12) Fill in the section, filling in every space, and cutting to fit as you go. Try and spread out your pottery designs if you are using more than one.

13) Now complete all the sections using the same methods.

14) Set aside the mosaic to dry. Grout the whole clock in the same session, but work in sections. Start on one section and apply grout, working it into each small crack. Don't worry if your grout goes into the central hole at this stage, we will chip it away once it has dried. Wipe away the excess grout and move on to the next. Repeat all the way around.

15) Scrub away the excess grout once it has fully dried. Use sandpaper (glass paper) to lightly sand all the way around the clock, so it has a smooth edge. Give the clock a thorough polish.

Suppliers

When purchasing tiles, most tile suppliers offer smaller sheets, or 'tester' sheets, for a fraction of the price of a whole sheet of tiles. Always look for this option, and if you can't see it on their website, give them a call. It's also worth mentioning that most mosaic suppliers use different names and descriptions for the same type of tiles.

In this list I have tried to give you the exact colours I used, however, so long as you have the right size tiles, the hue doesn't matter too much. The designs will still work. If in doubt, just choose a colour that you like.

AUSTRALIAN SUPPLIERS

www.mosaictiles.com.au

Iridescent tiles 1.5 cm (0.6 in):
Green (Green Opal), Light Blue (Sky Blue Opal), Dark Blue (Blue Azul Opal), Biege (Beige Opal)

Opaque tiles 2cm (¾ in)
Blue (Deep Blue Vetricolour)

www.ozmosaics.com.au/shop/

Iridescent tiles 1.5 cm (0.6 in):
Light Green (Smalto Glass Supremo S08 Seine), Pink (Smalto Glass Supremo S03 Ooooh LA LA), Black (Smalto Glass Supremo S17 Moody), Orange (Smalto Glass Supremo S07 Moulin)

www.ebay.com.au

Glitter tiles 2 cm (¾ in): Turquoise;
For Leponitt wheeled nippers, coasters, circles (magnets), apples, hearts, bird-shaped box, circular box, baubles, tree, 3D heart, and clock kit

www.ozmosaics.com.au/shop/

Opaque tiles 2 cm (¾ in)

Mirror tiles

Transparent tiles 2 cm (¾ in)
Light Green (GC79 Green Eyed Monster Vitreous Mosaic Tiles)

www.themosaicstore.com.au

Glitter tiles 2 cm (¾ in):

Purple (Purple Glitter Glass), Red (Red Glitter Glass), Pink (Pink Glitter Glass) Gold (Gold Glitter Glass), Orange (Orange Glitter Glass)

Opaque tiles 2 cm (¾ in):

Purple Mix (Purple Mix Venetian Glass), Purple (Purple Iridised Glass), Lilac (Light Purple Venetian Glass), Red (Red Venetian Glass). Yellow (Yellow Iridised Glass), Orange (Bright Orange Venetian Glass), Light Blue (Light Blue Venetian Glass), Black (Black Crystal Glass), Silver (Silver Silverfoil)

Transparent tiles 2 cm (¾ in):

Dark Green (Transparent Green Glass), Red (Transparent Red Glass), Blue (Transparent Blue Glass), Light Blue (Transparent Light Blue)

Pebbles

Blue (Mini Iridised Blue Glass Gems), Black (rounded), (Black Glass Droplets), Black (flat) (XL Black Glass Droplets)

www.belianamosaics.com.au/

For Leponitt wheeled nippers

www.cluttercraft.com.au

For the coasters

www.mdfmagic.com.au

For circles (magnets), apples, butterflies, and hearts

www.urbanwordsaustralia.com.au

For butterflies, hearts, and bunting

www.arbee.com.au

For the bauble

www.craft.com.au

For the bauble and the tree

www.amazon.co.uk

For the tray

www.letsmaketime.com.au

For the clock kit

www.ceramicraft.com.au

For the clock kit

UK SUPPLIERS

www.mosaictraderuk.co.uk

Iridescent tiles 1.5 cm (0.6 in):

Green (Quadra Opaline: Iridescent Magic – Arugula)

Glitter tiles 2 cm (¾ in):

Purple (Glitter Sparkle Crystal Emperor Purple), Red (Glitter Sparkle Crystal Heartbreak Red), Pink (Glitter Sparkle Crystal Fuchsia Magic), Turquoise (Glitter Sparkle Crystal Aztec Turquoise), Gold (Glitter Sparkle Crystal Gold Bullion), Orange (Glitter Sparkle Crystal Burnt Orange)

www.mosaicsupplies.co.uk

Iridescent tiles 1.5 cm (0.6 in):

Green (Sicis Iridium Mint 4 Dark Greens), Light Green (Sicis Iridium Fern 3 Greens), Light Blue (Sicis Iridium Iris 2 Lighter Blues), Dark Blue (Sicis Iridium Iris 4 Dark Blues), Biege (Sicis Iridium Zinnia 2 Beiges), Pink (Sicis Iridium Crocus 2 Soft Pinks), Black (Sicis Iridium Orchis Blacks), Orange (Sicis Iridium Dahlia 4 Orangey Reds).

Glitter tiles 2 cm (¾ in)

Mirror tiles

www.mosaictofit.co.uk

Iridescent tiles 1.5 cm (0.6 in):

Green (Jade Green), Light Green (Green Pearl), Light Blue (Moonstone Blue), Dark Blue (Sapphire Blue), Pink (Pink), Black (Jet Black) Orange (Orange)

www.hobby-island.co.uk

Glitter tiles 2 cm (¾ in)

Purple (Sparkle Crystal Emperor Purple), Red (Sparkle Crystal Heartbreak Red), Pink (Sparkle Crystal Fuchsia Magic), Turquoise (Sparkle Crystal Aztec Turquoise), Gold (Sparkle Crystal Gold Bullion), Orange (Sparkle Crystal, Burnt Orange), Lilac (A85 Pink Blush), Red (A96 Red), Yellow (A90 Bright Yellow), Orange (A93 Mandarin), Blue (A19 Blue Heaven), Light Blue (A12 Aqua), Black (A49 Black)

www.mosaictraderuk.co.uk

Opaque 2 cm (¾ in):

Purple Mix (Classic Mix Colour Mosaic – Rhodolite)

Mirror tiles:

Silver (Glitter: Sparkling Crystal Precious Metal Silver)

www.hobby-island.co.uk

Opaque 2 cm (¾ in):

Purple (A43 Violet)

www.mosaicheaven.com

Mirror tiles

www.hobby-island.co.uk

Transparent tiles 2 cm (¾ in):

Dark Green (Light Green), Light Green (Green), Blue (Blue), Light Blue (Dark Teal)

www.mosaic-workshop.co.uk

Transparent 2 cm (¾ in):

Dark Green (C730 Strong Green), Red (C99 Dark Red), Blue (C45 Mid Blue), Light Blue (C765 Light Blue); and for Leponitt Wheeled Cutter (tile nippers)

www.mosaictofit.co.uk

Pebbles:

Blue (Blue Opalescent Nuggets)

Black (rounded) (Black Marble Nuggets)

www.etsy.com

For Leponitt Wheeled Cutter (tile nippers)

www.ebay.com

For Leponitt and other brands available

www.homecrafts.co.uk

For the coasters

www.woodcraftshapes.co.uk

For the apples and circles (magnets)

www.craftlettersandshapes.co.uk

For the butterflies

www.craftshapes.co.uk

For the hearts

www.littlecraftybugs.co.uk

For the 3D heart, tray, tree, bauble, circular box, and bird box

www.ebay.co.uk

For the clock kit (230 mm French Spade Hands – Black), 3D heart, tray, tree, bauble, circular box, bird box, bunting, heart, butterflies, apples, coasters, and circles (magnets)

www.amazon.com

For the bunting

Templates

PEACOCK VASE (left)

Increase the template size to fit your vase.

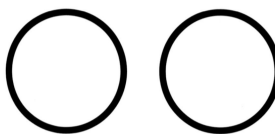

OWL LANTERN (above)

FLORAL TRAY (below)

MEADOW IN A BOWL (below)

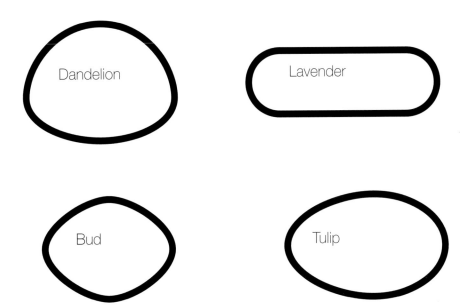

Dandelion

Lavender

Bud

Tulip

SUN CIRCLE HOUSE NUMBER (below)

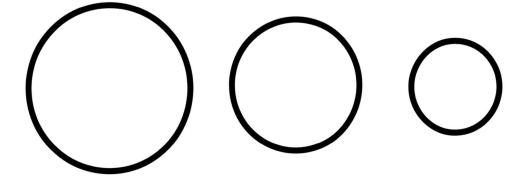

About the Author

Alice Vinten has been a lover of all things craft since childhood. Her passion for mosaic has developed during ten years of dedicated cutting, nipping, smashing and creating. She has sold commissioned mosaics across the UK and Europe, her work has been displayed in local art galleries and she has been complimented for her innovative use of light and colour. Her pieces are unique modern designs, made using traditional methods. Alice has written craft tutorials for UK magazines and runs a popular community craft page on Facebook. When she is not making, she is thinking about what she will make next. She has a strong desire to share her passion for mosaic with other craft lovers.

Alice is drawn to bright colours and sparkling reflections, an obsession fuelled by her love of Barcelona and all things Antoni Gaudi. She integrates a wide range of materials into her mosaics, including broken china, mirror and even re-purposed jewellery. She is a keen upcycler and delights in re-purposing unwanted items into beautiful ornaments.

Share your mosaic project pictures with Alice at
https://www.facebook.com/CraftyLoveUK and
http://wonderlandus.wix.com/-alicevinten

Dedication

To my wonderful husband, who has infinite faith in my talents, and to my two beautiful boys, Freddy and Arnie, who inspire me every day.

Special thanks go to David and Peter Vinten who have both kindly lent me their cameras during this project. Also thank you very much to my parents, Anna and Peter Hearn, and my mother-in-law, Janet Vinten, for providing my children with love and care while I was busy making and writing. Without the support of my loving family this book wouldn't have been possible. I would also like to thank New Holland Publishers for giving me the opportunity to write my first book. I hope it's the beginning of a long journey together!

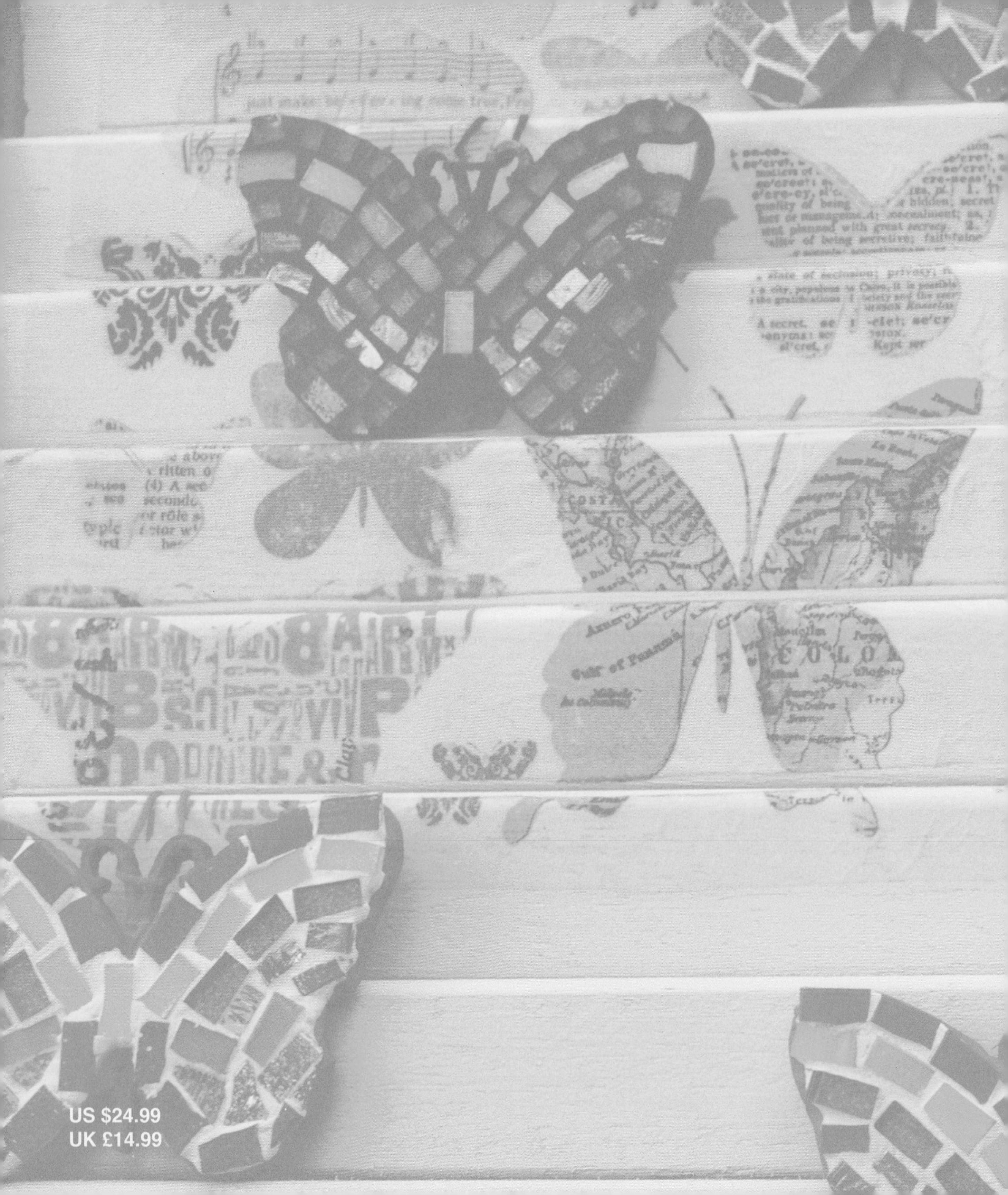

US $24.99
UK £14.99